ALSO BY
MARTIN FLETCHER

*Breaking News*

*Walking Israel*

*The List*

*Jacob's Oath*

*The War Reporter*

*Promised Land*

# TEACHERS
## *The Ones I Can't Forget*

## Martin Fletcher
### *foreword by* Tom Brokaw

NEW YORK

LONDON · NASHVILLE · MELBOURNE · VANCOUVER

# TEACHERS
*The Ones I Can't Forget*

Published in New York, New York, by Morgan James Publishing. Morgan James is a trademark of Morgan James, LLC. www.MorganJamesPublishing.com

Proudly distributed by Ingram Publisher Services.

A **FREE** ebook edition is available for you or a friend with the purchase of this print book.

CLEARLY SIGN YOUR NAME ABOVE

**Instructions to claim your free ebook edition:**
1. Visit MorganJamesBOGO.com
2. Sign your name CLEARLY in the space above
3. Complete the form and submit a photo of this entire page
4. You or your friend can download the ebook to your preferred device

ISBN 9781636981079 paperback
ISBN 9781636981086 ebook
Library of Congress Control Number:
2022950125

**Cover and Interior Design by:**
Jason Snyder

Morgan James is a proud partner of Habitat for Humanity Peninsula and Greater Williamsburg. Partners in building since 2006.

Get involved today! Visit: www.morgan-james-publishing.com/giving-back

# TEACHERS

*For those who said to me*

"Robbers stole my sister's leg."

ALBINO CHILD, TANZANIA

"Prisoner-of-War in Syria?
It was like a sanitarium after Auschwitz."

ISRAELI HOLOCAUST SURVIVOR

"Please don't tell my mother I smoke."

PALESTINIAN SUICIDE BOMBER, WEST BANK

"I want to be a pilot."

8-YEAR-OLD ORPHAN GIRL WITH HIV, UGANDA

"Can I have your pencil please?"

STARVING BOY, SOMALIA

# CONTENTS

# FOREWORD

MY LONGTIME FRIEND and colleague Martin Fletcher is a peerless journalist of the old school, wading through the bleakest corners of the world, especially in the Middle East and Africa, camera in hand, compassionate and curious.

His tireless passion for the tales that go well beyond the hit-and-run school of too much modern journalism is legendary in television news. It has won him almost every award in television journalism, many multiple times.

As a colleague, I'm always reassured when I see Martin's name on the travel manifesto.

In his quiet and caring manner, he takes us along with him—revealing everyday experiences that for decades made up his world of conflicts, large and small.

We were together in the tense struggle for survival in Mogadishu in East Africa. The Somali warlords were pretending to be compassionate because the United States was sending in relief for the dying locals.

Martin and I decided the most effective way of telling the story was to document a Mogadishu father, who had already lost his wife, desperately trying to save his malnourished daughter.

Martin stayed at his side as he lost what was a foreordained struggle.

His compassionate account was heartbreaking but essential to understand the madness of that conflict.

In these pages, you'll see again and again the journalism of a truth teller in desperate circumstances. Telling the revealing intimate stories that would go unnoticed without the heart and soul of this great journalist, who has a calling.

*Tom Brokaw*

"You will go from land to land
 Be the bleeding heart of the world
 Its screaming mouth…"

———————————

Hang on
Hold on,
Hold on tight
Hold in there,
How can I let go?
Don't let go
And if you let go
Experience the fall
Stand Up
And If you fall too deep
Learn to come back and
Grab yourself again
Hold on, hold on

# AUTHOR'S NOTE

THANK YOU, NBC NEWS for allowing me to travel the world and tell the stories of the people I met on your broadcasts. I hope we did some good. And thank you for allowing me access to your archives and permission to work with the images that follow.

The images that begin each chapter are digitally combined freeze frames created from my news reports on *NBC Nightly News* and *Today*. I feel that every good story can be summed up in one word and that word is usually an emotion. Conveying that emotion is my job, for that is what viewers connect with. A plane crash is not about tons of metal hitting the ground but fear, or pain, or sadness. A medical breakthrough is not about pills or syringes but relief or joy. A hurricane or flood is not about wind and water but homes and lives. And so with these images I try to distill an entire news report into one frame, one twenty-fourth of a second that says it all. One moment that conveys a world. The story is mine but the emotion is yours.

These eleven images, blown up in size, form a picture exhibit that will be shown across the country and beyond. This book tells their stories and a whole lot more.

# Fall Down Seven Times, Get Up Eight

I HAVE LONG WANTED to write a book about what I learned in my four decades of reporting, and of course joked it would have to be a very slim book.

I've certainly seen a lot. My business was to meet people on the worst day of their lives, tell their story, and move on, often to a different tragedy in a different country. I needed thick skin, but many left a scratch on my soul. I learned from their lives and they changed me.

It is from this well that I draw.

For our world is made of tiny stories. Some are happy and funny, some are tragic, some merely unfortunate.

We are told the road to success is paved with failure, for that is where the lessons are, these are the stories that help us grow. Well, that's where I come in.

Take the Greek women's relay team. In the 4 x 400 relay at the 2004 Athens Olympics, the United States women won gold,

Russia silver and Jamaica bronze. But the stadium's loudest cheer came a full half minute later when the last Greek runner finally fell across the finish line. While the press pounced on the victors, my attention was on the losers. Who were these Greek duds? How did it feel to fail so fully? Before their home crowd even?

All winners celebrate the same way. They leap and hug and laugh and drape themselves in the national flag before the cameras. But what do the losers do?

———————————

The people I learned from lost. They may have been defeated, scared, weak, alone, but none gave up. They put one foot before the other and then another in the hope that tomorrow would be a better day, however unlikely.

Like the mother who waved away her newborn because she hated the thought of bringing her son into war and exile. Yet two days later, in her freezing tent in Kosovo, I watched as she nursed her baby and beamed with joy. The father in Somalia whose wife and four daughters died of starvation, yet who still dreamed of going home to plant his crops, find a new wife, and sit under the tree. The little girl in Macedonia who lost her family yet never stopped smiling. Every day in the refugee tent she drew stick figures of her mother and father and after two months, found them again. All these people and a thousand more taught me never to give up hope, that every problem has a solution, and that if you don't find it, keep looking. And if you still can't find it, well, find another way. As the saying goes, a door closes and a window opens. The Japanese say, fall down seven times, get up eight. And the British wartime slogan was Keep Calm and Carry On.

Anyway, what choice do we have?

———————————

In these pages I want to introduce you to some of the people from whom I have learned, and maybe pass on some of their lessons. I emerged from many of my encounters bewildered, wondering how the people I met in such hard times could possibly recover and how they could pick up the pieces. Over many years, and in many places, their fortitude has made our world stronger, and their tiny stories have given me forbearance and understanding. Above all, they have made me grateful for what I have and shown how easily it can be taken away.

———————————

My first teacher is Evelyne, a sweet little girl in Uganda. Eight years old, Evelyne was an orphan and HIV positive, yet she was wise beyond her years. The cover of her schoolbook revealed everything, and wet my eyes.

# TEACHERS

Delux....the joy of success.

EXERCISE BOOK

NAME __KABATESI  EVA_____
SCHOOL _OF  STRUGGLE_____
CLASS _OF  HOPE_____ YEAR _2008___
SUBJECT_____

45 PAGES

KAMPALA 2008

*Evelyne, in the red shirt, eight years old, an orphan. Her parents died of AIDS, she is HIV positive. She makes her bed, cleans the floor, washes and irons her clothes and each day walks from the orphanage to school. On the cover of her school book she wrote, "School of Struggle" and "Class of Hope."*

# *Evelyne Kabatesi*

I KNELT BY HER SIDE and stroked her head and felt the rough weave of her cropped hair. In a tiny voice, barely above a whisper, Evelyne was telling me that every night she dreamed of her mother, who had died of AIDS. Her father had too. I felt her tremble. Her voice trailed off into silence. I stood as she took my hand and walked me to the next room, where she joined three friends sitting on the ground.

Dinnertime. First they were given a beaker of water and pills to fight their virus, for each of these little orphans was HIV positive. Then they waited patiently for their meal of rice, beans and fried onions, the same each night.

The children stared at the ground, looking sad and worn, grouped around an empty burlap US aid sack which served as a tablecloth. Their foreheads glinted in the dim light from the bare bulb above. Our presence, three strangers with big cameras, an NBC News crew, didn't help the mood. But how happy could they be in a dark room in a cramped home for abandoned or orphaned children, many of whom were sick.

Evelyne made her own bed, washed her own clothes and swept the floor. All the clothes she owned fit in one drawer, along with her schoolbooks. To reach her only shoes she had to climb on top of the cupboard. Yet you would have thought that she had been brought up in the finest of homes. She curtsied as she shook my hand and whispered thank you and please. When I took my leave and thanked her, she murmured, "You're welcome."

But her schoolbook revealed all. The slogan on the Delux cover proclaimed The Joy of Success, a rousing call to study and succeed, a rallying cry of promise for all the children of East Africa.

Evelyne knew better.

Where she was supposed to write the name of the school, Evelyne had written: "School of Struggle."

And for class she had written: "Class of Hope."

In seven syllables she summed up her life.

In her other exercise books she had filled in all the spaces with the same single word: "Angels."

How much pain and understanding she had crammed into her young life, which she was able to communicate in so few words. Hope was like the last flutters of the dying candle in her bedroom.

However, in school she dressed for success, with her uniform of dark green sweater with white braiding and matching green skirt, which she had ironed herself. She strolled arm in arm with her friends, as boys kicked a ball in the yard. When the bell sounded for class, most children ignored it at first, then slouched into the low building as if heading for a caning. While Evelyne almost smiled at the tolling of the bell and was first into her classroom to learn English. There she sat at her wooden desk in the front row and, with bright eyes locked on her teacher's lips, she chanted in unison with the other boys and girls, "We are beautiful."

I never forgot that little girl. I find Evelyne, with her sweet, shy smile, to be one of the most inspiring people I have ever met, wise way beyond her years. Decades later, her wisdom born of hardship stays with me, and I think of her often. I think of what she wanted. Her favorite subject was math, and she hoped to be an airline pilot so that she could fly far, far away.

———————————

Since the age of two Evelyne had lived in an orphanage founded by Noelina Namukisa. Noelina preferred the term foster home, however, because orphanage emphasized loss, while foster home implied new love.

Years earlier in the slums of Kampala, Noelina had met a destitute woman who wanted to kill her two little daughters because she was terrified they would follow her into a life of violent abuse, drugs and prostitution. "Better to drown them now than let them live like me," she told Noelina. "They have nothing to live for in this filthy hole. Bring me poison," she said, "so I can kill myself and my girls."

But Noelina refused and persuaded the mother to give up her children. She would look after them, maybe find them a suitable home. Noelina had a small house with a tarpaulin tied to a tree in the yard to shelter from the sun and rain, and those two little girls became her first foster children.

When I met Noelina years later, she had a complex of several small buildings and more than thirty children in her care, and she invited volunteers to teach sex education, sewing and other crafts. Children from the slum joined the orphans in the classes, learning a trade, sitting with rapt attention. They're full of hope, I thought, I wonder how long the flame will last.

And I wondered what had happened to the two girls whose mother wanted to kill them. Noelina smiled. "Come and see," she said.

We telephoned ahead and drove for half an hour to the outskirts of Kampala, far from the slum, to a college where two young women, Sonja and Loyei, came running into Noelina's arms, laughing and squealing in delight. The two girls, whose mother had wanted to poison them, had just graduated. They all hugged and jumped up and down and had tears in their eyes, and frankly, so did I.

———

Success, it is said, comes when preparation meets opportunity. But what if, unlike Sonja and Loyei, you're fully prepared but there is no opportunity? That's what I ran into some months later, driving in the Turkana desert of northern Kenya, when we spotted in the distance an isolated complex of low buildings surrounded by razor wire. We thought it must be a prison or an army camp. Trailed by billowing sand we approached along

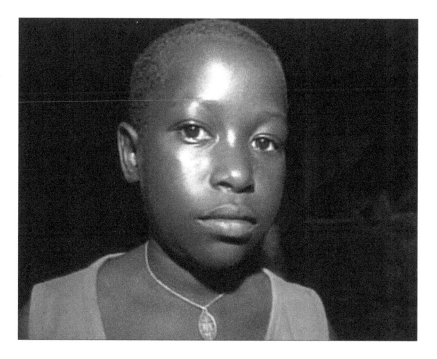

*Evelyne Kabatesi*

a dirt track and stopped at the locked main gate. There we saw a sign which took us by surprise: The Angelina Jolie Boarding School for Girls.

In the first classroom there was a geography test, so we went next door to the math class. With permission from the principal we talked to some of the girls. They had been selected as the brightest students from the nearby Kakuma refugee camp, at the time the largest refugee camp in the world, crammed with families who had fled war, famine and drought in Uganda, Somalia, Ethiopia, Sudan, and Burundi.

Kenyan police were posted at the entrance to the Kakuma camp, but despite their presence, at night the alleyways belonged to thugs who raped, stole and fought over girls and drugs. The lives of the young women were mapped out: fetchers of water and wood, makers of beds and meals, and by their mid-teens reluctant marriage and motherhood.

While at this boarding school, protected by razor wire and armed guards, two hundred and forty girls had earned the opportunity to live and study, and they grabbed it as if their lives depended on it, which they did. Here were school uniforms and regular meals, comfortable beds and supportive teachers, bright faces and ready laughter. In class the girls sat in twos at wooden desks and studied hard and raised their hands and spoke only when called upon.

A Hollywood grandee had helped to pluck these girls from a life of servitude and poverty and had revealed a world of possibilities. Nyanuel Noang, a fourteen-year-old refugee from Sudan, said that if she had still been in the Kakuma camp, by now she could have been married. Instead, she said firmly, "I want to be in school. I want to be a surgeon."

Her eleven-year-old friend Michu Gembula from Ethiopia, who reached her shoulder, wanted to be a math professor.

Their teacher smiled brightly. "They are determined," Rhoda Kiprotich said. "We teach them values, we hope their spirit will never die, and they will have hope to continue."

But continue how? The trouble was, when they graduated from this junior school, there was no senior school to go to. Rhoda could only wish that there was a secondary boarding school nearby, but there wasn't. Some of the students might find sponsors who would send them to a private boarding school elsewhere in Kenya, but for most of these bright, hopeful girls, full of talent and dreams, after graduation there was nowhere to go but back to their parents. There, back in the Kakuma refugee camp, returning to their destiny, their future was to make their brothers' beds and endure a quick forced marriage.

Of the tens of thousands of girls in the camp, a handful had glimpsed a future that could never be theirs. No doubt a few would find a way out, but the vast majority would revert to their traditional roles as servants to men. And that would be doubly hard, for just as they were about to take flight, their wings would be clipped. What a waste, I thought. I found it painful. What great potential there was here, and so few opportunities.

---

And worse, what about when there's neither preparation nor opportunity? Just hope—and that is dashed; the candle dies. Then what?

One of the worst memories of my life, and another painful lesson, is of a feeding station in Mogadishu, the capital of Somalia, where I extinguished the hope of a hungry boy.

All around me, people were dying of starvation at the rate of a dozen a day. As day broke we woke to the wailing of parents carrying the corpses of their infants to the makeshift cemetery across the road. It was hard to see, for we had no help to give to the mothers who looked at us with beseeching eyes. And as we moved uncomfortably among the hovels, I noticed that a little boy, about six years old, was following me, keeping a respectful distance. He had a distended belly and only isolated tufts of hair on his scalp. Everywhere I went, as I peered into shelters fashioned from twigs and straw and plastic, as I observed hundreds of children sitting on the ground being fed rice and beans and vitamin tablets, and walked past the orderly line of refugees waiting to see a nurse, there he was: the hungry boy, silent, patient. As he followed me he scratched at the bumps of scurvy beneath his skin.

Our eyes met. I offered him what I had. I held out a granola bar. He refused it. Bottled water. He ignored it. A sandwich. He looked away. I shrugged and went to see whether there was water in the tap. The day before there had been none. Then there was a wave of anticipation as a truck pulled up piled high with boxes, a donation from somewhere in Kansas. The hungry crowded around. Aid workers opened one box and then another and then another, shaking their heads in annoyance. The donation consisted of five thousand pairs of purple pants. What a waste of money for transport. Someone must have got a tax write-off for a charitable contribution and dumped a load of unsellable wares. The aid workers were dumbfounded. The refugees looked resigned. All the time I wrote in my notebook and all the time the little boy followed me. Again he declined. No food. No water. I thought of my own son, about the same age, who was always looking into the full fridge and complaining that there was nothing to eat. Finally, I asked my local guide Absame to ask the boy what he wanted.

Absame translated. "He wants your pencil."

"My pencil? That's all? But I've only got one," I said.

Absame spoke roughly to the child whose face crumpled. He seemed to shrink. He ran away, kicking up dust with his bare feet. "He won't bother you again," Absame said proudly. I watched the boy run away, throwing one last beaten glance over his shoulder as he disappeared among the starving and the sick.

That experience has haunted me ever since. Why didn't I give him my pencil? What, I couldn't find another one? But in the moment, trying to record the drama around me, and with only one pencil, I didn't see farther than my notebook.

I knocked the wind right out of that boy. I didn't see what a lowly pencil must have meant to a child suffering from starvation who nevertheless refused food and water and hungered only for something with which to write. More than anything, more than sustenance itself, he wanted to write. Or draw. Why? To study? To begin the long journey out of this hell? Was a pencil for him the missing link? How little would mean success for him.

His preparation could have begun with a simple little pencil. But I said No. Why? How was I so self-absorbed that although I had traveled thousands of miles to observe, I didn't understand what I was seeing? I tortured myself for days, I looked for him with a bundle of pencils from the NBC stores, but never found him. I hope he found another opportunity to get one, maybe from a kinder soul from CBS or ABC. And that he didn't lose his dream. I didn't get his name but that hungry, ambitious child is another harrowing scratch upon my soul, another teacher of mine.

Photo by IDF

## Gaza 2002

*Disfigured by fire, forsaken by her fiancé, Wafa chose the way
of the martyr. Taking Jews with her would give meaning to
her life, and her death. But when she pulled at the detonator,
the bomb in her pants didn't explode. She tugged again and
again and screamed in frustration and rage. Instead of going to
paradise she went to jail, where she sobbed and begged for mercy.*
I didn't kill anyone, *she cried,* please, please forgive me.

# *Wafa al-Biri*

IT IS A UNIQUE AND CHILLING MOMENT, frozen by an Israeli security camera: the instant a Palestinian suicide bomber, a young woman, pulls the detonator cord to blow herself up. Twenty pounds of explosives and iron nails are hidden in her pants. But the bomb didn't explode. Tugging again and again at the faulty charge, her face twisted to the sky, she screams in rage and frustration.

Wafa al-Biri's mission: travel from her Gaza home and blow herself up in Israel, in the Soroka hospital, killing Jewish doctors, nurses and patients. Instead she was stopped at Israel's border and arrested.

When he heard the news, Dr. Yuval Krieger couldn't believe it. He had fought so hard to save Wafa. Her Palestinian parents had even written a thank-you letter to his burn unit for their "warm and wonderful" care, saving the life of their 21-year-old daughter.

Dr. Krieger had an appointment with Wafa that day, but fortunately she didn't show up. For also expecting her were soldiers on duty at Erez, Israel's border crossing with Gaza. They had intelligence that a Palestinian suicide bomber was on the way, a female. And Wafa turned up.

The soldiers lured her into a small metal-fenced compound and ordered her through a loudspeaker to undress. That is when she realized that her mission had failed and in despair tried to kill herself. The soldiers seized the bomb and blew it up safely with a robot. So instead of going to paradise, as her handlers had promised, Wafa went to jail where she begged for mercy. "I didn't kill anyone," she cried, "please, please forgive me."

Why did a young woman, who had survived a serious kitchen fire, decide to sacrifice her life for the Palestinian cause? And of all targets, to pick a hospital, the very one that saved her life and treated her so well that her parents wrote with thanks. Latifa, a Palestinian friend who had spoken to Wafa every day for a month when Wafa was being treated for severe burns to her neck and arms, thought she knew the answer. "After her terrible burns Wafa's fiancé left her," Latifa said. "She felt abandoned and ugly. She cried and said she wanted to die. She said, "Somebody give me a bomb.""

The al-Aqsa Martyrs' Brigade obliged. The masked men offered martyrdom, a place of honor in heaven and money for her family. But Wafa's mother didn't want money, she wanted her daughter. "My daughter is sick," she told me. "They used her."

When the Palestinian suicide bombing campaign against Israeli civilians began in 1993, Israelis were horrified at the random violence and hatred, and tried to comprehend what they considered the incomprehensible: How could anybody hate so much that they were willing to die? The conclusion of

Israel's intelligence services at the time was that no more than a
dozen Palestinians fit the profile of a potential suicide bomber,
and as the well of politically motivated volunteers was therefore so shallow, the phenomenon would not last. The situation
was painful, it was crazy, but the intelligence services were sure
that only a few people were so mired in despair that they would
sacrifice their lives.

Ten years later, after a hundred and fifty suicide bombs,
or martyrdom operations as the Palestinians called them, the
Palestinian militias had so many volunteers they had to turn
them away. Very few were motivated purely by politics. Mostly
they sought revenge after Israeli troops had killed a loved one,
or felt desperation stemming from an upheaval in their lives, or,
especially among the youngest, were open to being persuaded by
evil people. Wafa was desperate after her scarring and the killers
spotted her vulnerability.

Israelis lived in fear or shrugged it off. Barbara Ruchames
could have been killed four separate times. Once, a bomb on a Tel
Aviv bus blew her off her bicycle. Another bomb exploded in a
Tel Aviv cafe as she walked by with her dog, and the dog was so
petrified Barbara had to carry him home. A bomb went off at an
ATM machine as she was checking the money in her purse. And
in Jerusalem, she was in the library of the Hebrew University
when a bomb exploded in the cafeteria next door. Total:
forty-three dead, one hundred and forty-seven wounded. Barbara
walked away without a scratch and still can't believe her luck.

I met a few bombers like Wafa—the failed ones, the ones
who lived. None of them was motivated purely by political
anger at Israel; there was always a more immediate, personal

reason. Hussam Abdu was angry at being short, Samir was depressed and felt his life was hopeless. Mohammed stands out, though, because of the incongruity of his goal, an innocent youth with murder on his mind. He was fifteen years old and looked thirteen. Soldiers at a roadblock thought he acted suspiciously, searched him at gunpoint and found a bomb strapped to his chest. "I came to kill the Jews," he said. Again, he was disarmed and the bomb exploded harmlessly, while he slumped on the sidewalk, hands handcuffed behind his back. A few days later I spoke to him while he was being interrogated by Shin Beth, Israel's domestic secret service.

But first I had met his mother, Delal, who told me not to listen to him. Militants had brainwashed her son. "They are criminals," she said, "these people who take children. God will punish them."

She took me to talk to his schoolmates, none of whom could believe that their friend could do such a thing. But they had noticed that members of al-Aqsa Martyrs' Brigades were hanging around after school and that Mohammed would get into their car. Delal wiped away tears. It was a difficult encounter for her and her son's friends. The boys didn't know where to look, but they listened respectfully and nodded knowingly when she told them, "Don't let anybody brainwash you, your mothers need you. Like I need my son."

I found Mohammed in a small whitewashed room, decorated with an Israeli flag, on an army base deep in the West Bank. He was downcast, his words barely audible, his voice that of a child. But his eyes lit up when I told him that I came with a message from his mother.

*Al-Aqsa Martyrs' Brigades*

As I read him the message, though, he shifted uncomfortably. It was a plea. "You should depend on God and confess. Boy, please, tell the Israelis everything, tell them who sent you."

He did. Al-Aqsa. He told me that at first he had refused to carry a bomb into Israel, but the al-Aqsa fighters kept talking and talking, saying he would be a martyr and God would forgive him. In the end he agreed. He couldn't explain why and said he was afraid.

By now Mohammed's slight frame was doubled over as he wiped tears from his eyes. He took nervous puffs from a cigarette that a guard had given him and blew the smoke over his shoulder, away from me. He lit a second cigarette with the butt of the first.

I kept thinking how young he was, how gullible, how unprepared for the hardships to come. He faced many years in prison, for bomb-running and attempted murder. He had sacrificed his youth. For what?

But for him that wasn't the worst of it. What truly alarmed Mohammed was when I told him that I would report back to his mother.

"What?" he said. "You're going to see my mother again?"

"Yes," I answered. "I promised I'd let her know how you are. Show her a photo."

"Oh no. No," he said, eyes wide with fear. "Please. Please don't tell my mother I smoke."

I promised Mohammed and kept his guilty secret.

Delal was touched that we had taken the trouble to return with news of her son, and served us coffee and cake. But when we hooked up to her TV and showed her the video of Mohammed in the interrogation room, she broke down. He looked haunted, pale, frail and helpless, tears glistening in his eyes. Dalal froze, her lips quivered, then with a cry she leapt across the room and hugged the television set and wouldn't let go.

We decided to find al-Aqsa and ask them directly: Why did you recruit a fifteen-year-old child to kill himself? Locating them wasn't difficult because we already knew their leaders in Balata on the edge of Nablus. It is the largest refugee camp in the West Bank, with about twenty-five thousand people crammed in an area of about one square mile, a maze of alleys, crumbling dark homes, open sewage and countless children who follow you, shouting and jeering.

We found one of the leaders, Nasser Abu Aziz, who himself had been jailed at the age of thirteen. He walked openly through the streets with an AK-47 Kalashnikov automatic rifle slung over his shoulder, a dog tag around his neck, wearing an olive green shirt with the word "Police" on his breast. He swore they had not given Mohammed the bomb. "We'd never send a child to his death," he said.

"So who did give the boy the bomb to kill the Jews?" I asked.

"Maybe it was the Israelis."

Yeah, right. I knew it had to be Alaa Sanakreh, Nasser's boss, or someone like him, one of the other leaders of the al-Aqsa brigades in Nablus. Sanakreh was near the top of Israel's Most Wanted list. Obsessed with security and surrounded by bodyguards, he slept in a different bed each day after patrolling the camp's alleys by night. I knew where to find him: at Um Alaa's, his mother's. I had already visited him several times.

Alaa Sanakreh had jet black hair, piercing dark eyes and chiseled cheekbones that framed an immobile olive face. He was a terrorist to the Israelis, a freedom fighter to the Palestinians and an impeccable source to me. He was a militant to whom I turned for understanding and comment at each violent twist of the Palestinian intifada, or uprising, against Israel.

His brother Ahmed, baby-faced with black hair sticking up in gelled spikes, was an expert bomb maker. Before anyone else, Israel wanted him dead. One afternoon a clutch of Sanakreh's henchmen burst through the door of their mother's house, dragging Ahmed, who had been shot in a clash with Israeli soldiers. He had three small entry holes near his stomach and needed urgent medical attention, but they didn't dare take him to the hospital, where the soldiers could find him. It had become almost routine. Ahmed had been shot eight times by Israeli soldiers—in the head, the jaw, the chest, the back, the stomach, a leg, an arm and one hand. His mother, well-practiced, rushed in and out with cloths and boiling water.

When they left, presumably for a doctor's private home, and the commotion had died down, Um Alaa refilled our glasses. For we had become so familiar with the terrorist's family that when they burst in we had just arrived for tea with their mother. This was the ninth time Ahmed had been shot, and his luck ran out. A few days later he would die.

But that's how well I came to know Alaa Sanakreh, one of Israel's greatest enemies. And even though I was aware of Stockholm Syndrome, nevertheless, I thought he was a pretty good guy. Mauling Shakespeare's insight that "Some are born great, some achieve greatness, and some have greatness thrust upon them," I always wondered whether Alaa Sanakreh was born a terrorist, strived to become a terrorist, or was forced by circumstances to become one. After all, he was just fighting to defend his people. I certainly didn't approve of his methods, like giving his brother's bombs to schoolboys, but I understood his motives.

While he was on the run, in two dozen encounters, I never saw him smile. He knew that he would eventually be killed, and so would Ahmed, that they would never marry or have babies. So they refused to allow their youngest brother Ibrahim to join the struggle. He was the designated survivor, the one to study hard in school and look after their mother and continue the family line. The only time I saw Alaa show any emotion was a short time later. His greatest fear had been realized.

Ibrahim heard one night, wrongly, that Alaa had been shot. He ran out into the deserted dark streets, breaking the curfew, looking for his brother, and ran straight into an Israeli army patrol. They shot him dead.

Now Alaa was the only surviving son and he'd had enough. What he most wanted, even while still coordinating attacks against Israelis, was peace. He wanted to marry Jasmine, a student at An-Najah National University in Nablus. He wanted a family. But her parents wouldn't hear of it. They said they didn't want a corpse for a son-in-law.

So when I found Alaa Sanakreh to ask him about the schoolboy, Mohammed, maybe his answer should not have surprised me. Of course, like his friend Nasser, he denied he had anything to do with recruiting a schoolboy, but then, for the first time, he told me he had had enough. "Martin, you saw with your own eyes my brother die," he said. "I tried to save him, but they killed him, Allah bless him. Do you think I wanted my brothers to die? I don't want more Intifada."

Some time later Palestinian leaders ordered their fighters to lay down their arms. They were working on a peace agreement with Israel and wanted quiet in the territories. Sanakreh accepted Israel's offer of an amnesty and got a job—as a policeman, an officer in the Palestinian Preventive Security unit. He could sleep in the same bed at night.

Even better, he got to share that bed with Jasmine, after her parents relented, secure in his newfound status. He moved out of the refugee camp and into a two-bedroom apartment in town, closer to the university where his new wife was studying for her MA in political science.

When I next visited, Jasmine, wearing jeans and a scarf to cover her hair, was holding her one-month-old son Ahmed while Alaa chased their two-year-old daughter Bana around the room. He never stopped grinning.

He had swapped bombs for babies, death for diapers, and it was clear how relieved he was. When he began to tell me about his life fighting the Israelis Jasmine's hand shot into the air, as if smacking it, and with a glare she silenced him. "She hates to hear about that part of my life," Sanakreh said with a happy smile.

I nodded. I had wanted to ask him, now that he lived in peace and quiet with his own young family, whether he ever thought about the Palestinians he had sent to their deaths. Did he think of the Jews he had killed? Some of them were little children like his. But I didn't have the heart.

He had learned his lesson. He had found his peace. Why disturb it?

## JERUSALEM 1995

*It must have been lonely inside the head of Rasha—blind, severely autistic, barely able to talk, abandoned by her parents at the age of six. But when Christian missionaries took in the Moslem child, a Jewish piano teacher changed her life. Now, hunched over the piano, fingers dancing to the music that is her world, Rasha laughs with joy.*

# *Rasha Hammad*

RASHA HAMMAD SAT SILENT and alone for hours at a time, for years. Until one day, when she was eleven years old, with a catchy tune playing on the radio, Rasha began to hum along to the music, tapping out the rhythm, her head nodding in time. It was the first time she had seemed to communicate since her parents abandoned her five years earlier.

The Christian missionary carers gathered, surprised. Could music be the breakthrough? They sensed that here, at last, was a way to enter Rasha's mind, to communicate with the blind, autistic girl who rocked to and fro in the corner. And they thought, who knows, maybe she has real musical talent too. So the missionaries contacted a music teacher. It was Deborah Schramm, an orthodox Jew, and there began a friendship that defied all odds.

Every Thursday for years, Dutch missionaries guided Rasha through the Israeli roadblocks, where she had special permission to pass from the Arab West Bank to the Jewish side of Jerusalem, to the home of the Jewish piano teacher.

And slowly and gently, by manipulating Rasha's fingers on the piano keys, teacher and pupil established a bond of trust.

From Do, Re, Mi, Rasha graduated to Chopin and Rachmaninoff, and one day she surprised her teacher by playing something she had not taught her. "It was Brahms' second movement of the Third Symphony," Deborah recalled. Rasha had heard it on the radio.

Sometimes their piano lessons were interrupted by gunfire, when Palestinians from Rasha's home in Bet Jala fired at the Jews in Gilo, on the edge of Jerusalem, and Israeli soldiers fired back. The fighting often lasted for days. Deborah would phone the Christian charity to make sure Rasha and the other children were safe. And the Moslem helpers who worked with the Christian missionaries there would pray for Deborah's Jewish family.

One day, when the shooting stopped, I was leaning against Deborah's living room wall, admiring Rasha at the piano, when suddenly, in an explosion of joy, she threw her head back, her eyes gleamed, and her smile became a wild grin as her fingers skipped and danced along the keys. And I thought: with all the hatred around, all it takes to save a child is a few kind souls.

---

Only twenty miles away, across the hills and valleys, it was a dark, chilly start to a day to remember. Palestinian children, in their best warm clothes, emerged from their homes and came in ones and twos to a waiting bus in the village square. Dawn was breaking when they climbed aboard, dim light over the eastern peaks creasing the blue-black night. "It's been my dream," twelve-year-old Odai said, taking his seat with a shy smile.

When roadblocks and other barriers were lifted on the West Bank, permitting easier travel for Arabs, a group of Israelis and Palestinians, all former fighters done with bullets and bombs, decided they would treat some Palestinian children and bring them to the beach in Israel. The boys and girls had spent all their lives in a village sixty miles from the coast. From their homes in the hills they could see the sunset, admire the flaming orange ball sinking into the shimmering blue Mediterranean Sea; so near and yet so far. For they had never dipped their toes in its waters.

Odai had promised his father he'd bring him a seashell. The day had turned hot now, 105 degrees Fahrenheit, but the children couldn't sit still, pointing, singing, clapping, and calling all the time, like boys and girls everywhere, "Are we there yet? How much longer?"

When the slice of shifting blue expanse appeared between apartment buildings taller than anything they'd ever seen, they shouted with joy. The children poured from the bus and ran to the beach, flinching as the hot sand scalded their soles. They laughed as the warm water tickled their toes. But after the lecture on how to stay safe in the water, Odai hesitated. He walked off by himself, head bowed, scanning the sand, looking for a seashell for daddy. He found four, put them aside for safekeeping and at last pulled the blow-up safety ring over his thin shoulders.

He paused at water's edge. He was suddenly hesitant. He had been told there was a whale in the water. But all around he could see men and women bathing and boys and girls on

*Oda*

paddleboards and a man carrying a box selling popsicles. Odai sucked in his breath, his shoulder blades protruding as his body straightened, and bravely let the water lap over his toes, which squished in the sand as the water covered his whole foot. Frowning, he took one step and then another until the water came up to his knee, whereupon, throwing caution to the wind, he sat down in the water. He smiled and laughed and smacked the waves with his hands. Arabic cries of joy from his village friends mingled with the Hebrew voices of the townspeople.

Around him Arab and Jewish volunteers hugged and congratulated each other.

Building bridges for peace.

## Kosovo 1994

*The sun rose, the sun set, it didn't matter much. From frigid to freezing, hungry to starving, diseased to dying— whatever; there was nowhere to go. Hungry, tired, sick, everyone looking for someone, and there was one girl with a blanket and the blank eyes of infinite pain.*

# Yehona

I COULDN'T STOP STARING. She was maybe sixteen years old, clutching a grey blanket to fight off the wet cold. It covered her head and body like a hijab, framing her still face. She looked straight at me, and through me, and finally looked away. After battle, soldiers have that thousand-yard stare, but I had never seen it on a child. I wondered if the woolen blanket itched her skin. And then I lost her in the crowd.

In that field there was no food, no water, no chair to sit on, nowhere to sleep, nowhere to relieve oneself. Fifty thousand Kosovars fleeing from the Serbs, dumped in a field, all doors closed to them, front and back, stuck in no-man's-land between Kosovo and Macedonia. Children cried, parents despaired, mothers gave birth, old people died. Everyone was looking for someone, families divided, loved ones lost in the crush.

And then the rain fell, hard, drops like fists. It bounced in the puddles. People drank from their hats and huddled under sodden coats and slithered in the mud.

Only when the sun began to set, and grayness settled over the shambles, did the rain stop. An old woman gripped her worn face in disbelief, a little boy walked alone and wailed. When night set in, so came the silence, broken by coughing and cries from across the field for a doctor.

And later we met Yehona, a little five-year-old girl who had been lost in the crowd for days. She had wandered off looking for a quiet place to relieve herself, and in the teeming, squalid mass couldn't find her mother or her brothers and sisters again. Sheltered by aid workers, Yehona drew stick figures of her mother and father and put a smile on the face of everyone she met. But she also drew tears as she sat on a woman's knee and put her own words to a Kosovar folk song: "Oh, Mummy, where are you? Do you hear me, oh Daddy? Don't leave me alone like this."

When the Serb army attacked, the Moslems had fled. Yehona, her brothers and sisters and mother, who had just given birth, joined the two-week-long slog through the mountains, enduring hunger, thirst, rain and bitter cold. Yehona's father stayed behind to fight. Nobody knew whether he was dead or alive.

After a week the field was cleared and many of the refugees were bussed or flown to host nations across Europe, while the remaining Kosovars gathered in refugee camps near Macedonia's capital, Skopje. That's where a British army captain gave Yehona a cot in the corner of his tent. He had taken a shine to this sweet face in the crowd. Each night, a different woman sang Yehona to sleep, as she clutched a doll with golden hair. Despite everything, she always fell asleep with a smile.

Captain Bob Soper called her the Face of Kosovo. She had green eyes, short chestnut hair, a thin pixie face, and an impish grin. Soper swore to find her family and made up a black-and-white poster of Yehona, now looking sad and lost, and placed copies in refugee camps all across the region, asking anybody who knew her to call him.

As the weeks passed his army duties took over and he had to find someone else to look after the forlorn little girl. One woman volunteered, and when Captain Soper brought Yehona to tent D-258 in Stankovic 1 refugee camp, Fatima Cecelia stroked her head, kissed her, then ducked inside to emerge with a photo in a plastic wrapper. More misery. It showed her own little children, a boy and girl with embroidered Moslem skull-caps, about Yehona's age. "Have you seen them?" she pleaded. "I lost them two weeks ago."

It was a heartbreaking time, as hundreds of thousands of Kosovo Moslems found refuge in neighboring countries, while the Kosovo Serbs burned and looted their homes. Ethnic cleansing, they called it. One group kicking out the other group to purify their homeland.

The world looked on in horror. The media poured in, intrigued by a refugee crisis in the heart of Europe. White people. But how fleeting is our view. It has been written that news coverage is like the beam of a lighthouse. It illuminates the darkness intensely and briefly, a blinding light, then the beam moves on to the next story, leaving behind the darkness. In the extended timeline of regional conflicts, we barge in and pass judgment on whatever we see happening directly before us, while seeking a simple narrative: Moslems good, Serbs bad. Indeed, it was cruel and tragic. But it was only part of the story, the part on which we shone our camera lights. The Serb atrocities and murders of

Moslems in Croatia, Bosnia and Kosovo were horrific, but for the Serbs it was payback time. The Moslems had done the same to the Serbs for much longer, for centuries, when the Islamic Ottoman Empire ruled the lands with whip and sword.

Then came World War I, the collapse of the Ottoman Empire, followed by the spread of communism, the creation of Yugoslavia, its breakup, and next—revenge. In reality, it was simply the turn of the Serbs, after hundreds of years of oppression. The slave, well-tutored, turned on the master. That's when we came in, cameras whirring, shining our lights, proudly writing what we love to call the first draft of history.

Tell all that to Yehona. She played ball with children in the camp and threw it right onto the tip of the nose of an older boy. I flinched and thought he would smack her, but they both laughed gaily and he chased the ball and kicked it back to her. When she comforted another girl crying for her parents, Yehona said, "Don't cry, I lost my father too and I'm not crying. He'll find you."

I imagine that rarely has a lost child been so brave. But every time I asked Yehona how she felt, she said: "I'm cold." And she would show me by taking my hand to pat her skin.

---

One country over, near Kosovo's border with Albania, Esak too was looking for his family. He was desperate to find out: Did he have a son or a daughter? On the first day that NATO troops entered Kosovo to stop the bloodshed and forced expulsions, NATO warned the refugees not to come home yet. They needed roads free for their tanks and troops, and they warned of booby traps and land mines laid by the Serb army. The women and children stayed in the camps waiting for the word, but their men ignored the orders. They swarmed the roads, walking and in cars, thousands of them, anxious to discover whether their homes still stood and who had survived the war.

But one lone man was walking the other way, not into but out of Kosovo. He seemed, if anything, more determined than the rest, head down, shouldering his way against the tide. His trousers were held up by rope and his jacket hung off his gaunt frame. His shoes didn't match.

His name was Esak and he had been taken prisoner two months earlier by the Serbs, forced into slave labor on the farmland lining the road. They made him dig holes in the fields to bury land mines. "Watch your step," he told us, pointing across a field to low hills. "That's where the mines are." It was a pastoral sight, with red-roofed homes and rickety barns nestling at the foot of green hills with cows grazing in an open field. He barely finished his warning when there was a blast of smoke followed by a loud explosion, maybe two hundred yards away, and parts of a cow flew ten feet into the air. "Every day a few cows are killed," he said. Dogs raced up and tore at the carcass.

Esak turned back to me and said bitterly, "I don't care about the beatings. But I can never forgive the Serbs for taking two months of my life and not letting me be at the birth of my baby." It was hard to see his pain. I nodded, laid my hand on his shoulder, unable to speak.

So we abandoned our big consequential report on the NATO convoy of German tanks entering Kosovo, even though it was Germany's first real use of its military might since World

War II. It faced a potential clash with the Serb army. It could mean war. So we turned around, all in favor of a more intimate concern: did Esak have a boy or a girl?

We parked the minibus at the entrance to the camp, and within a minute, Esak was hugging and pumping the hand of a friend. Moments later a balding, white-haired man with an impressive mustache fell upon him. "You're alive, you're alive," he wept, clutching Esak to his breast. "Oh, thank God, my son, you are alive." Esak swept his father into the air and couldn't talk. When he collected himself, he said, "Have you seen my wife? My new baby?"

"No," the old man replied. But he had heard that a few refugees were outside the camp staying in a nearby village. "Maybe try there?"

Close to half a million refugees from Kosovo had fled to Albania, their ethnic home. Of these, about a third had moved on to other countries in Europe, including Scandinavia, and even further afield, to America and Canada. The rest were divided among locations across Albania, as different communities absorbed as many as they could support. The earlier arrivals were the first to be moved on, and it had been months since Esak had seen his wife. He was biting his lip, his stoic face beginning to crumple. His only option was to find the aid organizations to ask if they had a list of names and destinations.

"May as well try the village first," I said. And so we set off again, driving for about thirty minutes. We stopped at a small roadside store to stock up on food and drink, as well as buy a little woolen cap. "For the baby," I said. "I have a hunch."

It wasn't much of a village, just a handful of brick structures with tin roofs set by an orchard of apple and blooming almond trees. The sweet fragrance may have been an omen. For when we climbed out of the vehicle, led by Esak, who kept calling out the name of his wife, Fatmire, which means good fortune, the head of a woman with jet black hair appeared from behind a door. Her hand flew to her mouth, the other clutched at her dress. Without saying a word she backed into the room and a moment later reemerged, holding a tiny baby swaddled in white, her arms outstretched as with an offering.

A neighbor couldn't contain herself and blurted out the name: "Fatma!"

Esak had a daughter who was four weeks old.

Hollywood couldn't have planned it better, I thought, and now the Big Hug. But life doesn't follow the script, and as I waited for the grand finale, the climax of our love story, it didn't come. Esak stood speechless, fixed to the ground, turned into stone by his emotions, five feet from his family. It was a beautiful tableau, a true still life, and a lousy TV moment. There would be no hug or kiss, not that we would see, at least.

But it was the truth, raw and real, an instant of awe. Esak had cheated death, and given new life. He had been alone and frightened and now he was whole. In that moment he became a man again, a husband, a father. What had happened to their house in Kosovo? Was its roof destroyed? Its contents stolen? Who cared? If home is where the heart is, Esak was home.

Smiles don't come much broader as Esak took Fatma and pointed at her and kept saying, "My baby! My baby!"

When he handed Fatma back to his wife her hands shook so much she couldn't hold her child. Her hands squeezed and rolled and wrung the woolen baby cap.

Word spread and all the neighbors and the dozen refugees came to celebrate the reunion, a rare happy ending. We left the young family sitting on thick grass under leafy trees with Esak's last words echoing in my head: I have survived.

———————————

As for Yehona, even when the war and the bombing ended, Captain Soper never gave up on his personal mission to find her parents. He had registered Yehona with the Red Cross, her name was on top of the list of seventy children separated from their parents, and he printed more posters to spread across the region.

Finally, several weeks later, a man heard about the little girl whose face was on all the bulletin boards and realized she was his niece, the daughter of his brother who had disappeared in the fighting. He drove the ten miles to the camp and collected Yehona, who suddenly became shy, confused and uncertain. She didn't want to leave her protectors but couldn't refuse a vanilla ice cream.

That night, Yehona, cheerful throughout her ordeal, was exhausted, her eyes red and strained. Dragging two small plastic bags with all her possessions, she could barely hold herself upright to enter the house in the Macedonian capital and meet her cousins for the first time.

*Yehona*

A week after that in Albania, Captain Soper at last found Sadie Aliu, who had lost Yehona two months earlier, when her daughter, shy about her needs, had wandered off, never to return.

"I used to cry for her," she said. "I saw her in my dreams. Yehona told me, Don't cry, mummy, I'm okay." Reunited in their home in a farming village, thanks to a caring British army captain, mother and daughter couldn't stop kissing each other. Yehona ran and played with her older brother and sisters and hugged and kissed the baby boy who she hadn't seen since he was two weeks old.

And then, the best news of all. In walked Sherif, Yehona's father, safe and well. He was short, powerfully built with graying hair and unshaven. He had spent the war hiding in the mountains, fighting with the resistance. He'd watched from the hills as the Serbs burned his town, but miraculously his own house had emerged unscathed.

————————————

The family faced a difficult winter. They had no electricity, no running water, and when NBC News visited, dinner for seven consisted of white bread dipped into a thin broth. But there was much laughter and they were thankful for what they did have: a family, and freedom.

The last we saw of Yehona she was swinging on the wooden gate of her home, singing to herself in English, words that she had probably learned from Captain Bob. She sang over and over: "How are you? How are you? I'm fiiiine, thaaank yooouuuu."

And Sadie was thankful that her daughter seemed unaffected by her ordeal. She said she was the same jolly child she had been before the war. But there was one strange thing, Sadie said. It didn't matter where Yehona was: in bed, by the fire, in the sun; she always felt cold.

## JERUSALEM 2002

*With bombs and guns and knives
they tried to kill the Jews. The
unthinkable was almost routine in
this ER built for traffic accidents,
but now a world leader in trauma
medicine.* I fight death, *the doctor
said.* I save lives and I cry.

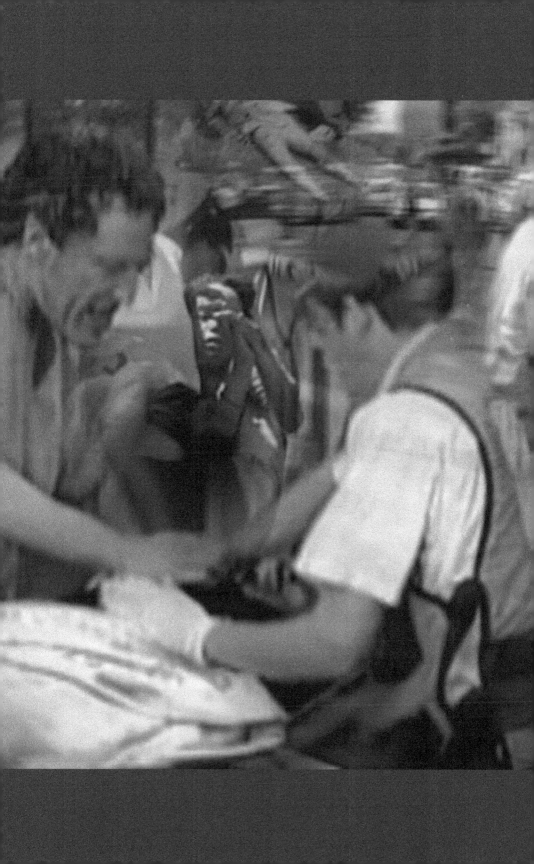

# *Avi and Nurit*

AS SOON AS THE WHEELS of the gurney hit the ground the doctor, on the move, began pumping the victim's heart. Every second counted. After each bomb attack dozens, even hundreds, of dead and wounded descended onto the emergency room of Hadassah hospital in Jerusalem.

And always at the arrival bay, marshaling the injured and calling out orders, was the same rugged doctor in green scrubs, handsome in a beat-up way, with chestnut curls, a strong somewhat misaligned jaw and powerful hands. Who is he? I wondered. He was like a field marshal commanding his troops, and the emergency room was like a battlefield, but here, the battle was to save lives, not take them.

The man in green directed the stretchers to the appropriate bay in the ER, making the first snap decisions: who could be saved, who could not. What should be done, and by whom. The worst moment, he said later, was when that ambulance door opened. Who is it? "Once you open the door—who is there?

That's the big question. It can be family, it can be a neighbor, it can be, God forbid, someone very close to you."

Jerusalem had become ground zero for terrorist bombers, and over a decade, Dr. Avi Rifkind, head of Hadassah's trauma unit, became the world's most experienced doctor in dealing with terror, or as he put it more technically: "We are experts in blood trauma." It was a grim claim to fame for the son of Holocaust survivors.

His unit had been established to handle traffic accidents and its operation was pretty tame until the mid 1990's, when the Palestinian struggle against the Israeli army suddenly exploded into a murderous campaign against civilians. The aim of the bombers and their masters was to kill and maim as many Jews as possible. The bombs exploded almost weekly, sometimes daily, even twice a day.

Palestinian bomb makers created innovative packages of death: explosives packed with thousands of nails, or tiny round steel ball bearings and bolts and screws, sometimes mixed with rat poison. They left them in backpacks and shopping bags in Jerusalem's restaurants, buses and pedestrian malls. As they pulled the detonator cord or pressed the button taped to their finger, the most devoted yelled *Allahu Akhbar*, God is Great, and blew themselves up among crowds of Israelis. Outgunned Palestinians proudly called the suicide bombers their own F-16 warplanes. They plastered their towns with dashing posters of their heroes, the martyrs, bedecked with guns and bandannas posing to the backdrop of Jerusalem's golden Dome of the Rock.

Each new bomb demanded new forms of treatment. One fourteen-year-old girl was stretchered in with hundreds of holes in her body. She was bleeding to death. Rifkind said the bomb had been laced with rat poison, an anticoagulant. As fast as she bled out, the doctors gave her new blood, but her body kept ejecting it. She was dying on their table. As a last resort they gave her a product that had not yet been approved by the U.S. Food and Drug Administration. There was nothing to lose, Dr. Rifkind said. "We gave her one shot of NovoSeven and she stopped bleeding. It was an experiment. It was amazing. And she survived."

On-the-job training as the unthinkable became almost routine.

A border policeman two months into his job, Shimon Ohana was eighteen years old when he died for twenty-five minutes. A Palestinian had shot him twice in the heart. He was pronounced dead at the scene. But after a quick consultation with Rifkind, medics zipped him into a body bag and rushed him to the hospital, where the trauma surgeon got to work. He opened the body bag, massaged the heart, sewed up the bullet holes, and poured in adrenalin, while colleagues thought he was being both cruel and foolish. But Rifkind persisted. And within a year, Shimon Ohana married and had a son.

Yet even Rifkind admitted that the sight of the victims was terrifying.

In that sense, those who wanted to sow terror had succeeded. Jerusalem became a city of nervous wrecks, of parents terrified to send their children to school, shoppers terrified to go to the market, passengers afraid to set foot on a bus.

Some sought refuge in the coastal towns of Tel Aviv and Netanya, but that didn't do much good. The bombers followed them there. There were bombs on buses, in nightclubs and cafes, in malls and outside schools. Word came down from the Prime Minister's office and became the country's refrain: Carry on as usual. Don't let the terrorists change your way of life.

———————

So after Islamic terrorists took three thousand American lives at the World Trade Center, and others stuffed letters with anthrax and mailed them to victims, and fear hit America square in the gut, it was to the long-suffering Jews of Jerusalem that some Americans turned for guidance.

Jake in Philadelphia urgently asked his sister Tsippi in Jerusalem for help. She had lived for years with the daily threat of stabbings, shootings, car bombs, bus bombs, train bombs, suicide bombs. "How do you do it?" he asked. "How do you live knowing your own body, and your childrens' bodies, have become the ultimate battlefield? Simply put: How do you live with terror?"

From the Middle East Tsippi responded caustically to her brother in middle America: "I can't believe I have to worry about YOUR safety." First of all, she said, calm down!

And the charming grandmother, short, frail-looking but tough as nails, sent an email listing how to live with the constant threat of terror, lessons she had learned the hard way. She worked as a therapist in Jerusalem schools, and she said that the worst hour in her life was when she attended the funeral of one of her pupils. The girl had been blown up by a suicide bomber who exploded himself in a crowded downtown pizzeria at two o'clock on a hot summer's day. He killed fifteen innocent people and wounded one hundred and thirty.

Tsippi gave practical advice. Warnings like *"Teach your children to avoid touching any object found on the sidewalks."* A bomb could be hidden inside a loaf of bread, inside a toy or a backpack. *"Be alert."* One woman spotted a man dressed like an orthodox Jew wearing a backpack, but the pack was of a kind, she said later, that Jews would never wear. She called the police, who stopped the man and found a bomb.

*Shop in the market as early as possible, before the crowds.* "Terrorists don't go to the market at seven o'clock in the morning," Tsippi wrote. "It takes them time to get there and there's nobody there, so it's not worth it for them."

And my favorite item in her list of living with terror: *"Israel must be one of the few countries in the world where parents actually encourage their children to play video games."* The reason: "it keeps them from playing in the streets and at home, where it's safer."

She ended her letter to Jake saying he should give his children a big goodbye kiss every morning. "Good luck! Love, Tsippi."

––––––––––––––

Tsippi wasn't the only Jewish woman busy at the computer with concerns about how to live with terror. She was answering a question but across town, forty-year-old Idit Shemer was asking one. "How," the frightened mother asked via the internet, "could Palestinians justify killing Israeli civilians?" Most responses were hostile and angry. But one stood out. It was from another mother, a Palestinian only twelve miles away, in Ramallah on the West Bank.

The two mothers, Idit and Najwa, corresponded for months and their concern for each other grew, softening a little the pain around them.

"I really worry about you," the Israeli wrote.

"Let me know that you and your children are okay," the Palestinian answered. Najwa Sadeh, forty years old, described the fear she lived with daily in Ramallah, how the constant presence of Israeli soldiers with guns traumatized her children.

Idit was learning what life must be like for the Palestinians, about the source of their fury and frustration. That didn't make life easier or safer, though, for either woman.

We got a taste of that when we were standing in the street with Idit and her phone rang. Her face contorted, and she hunched over her cellphone and pressed it into her ear. "Don't go outside, don't go outside," we heard her repeat, fear in her eyes. Her daughter was on the line. A bomb had exploded at the gate to her school. She couldn't leave. The police were there. Her voice shook.

Since that near miss, each time Idit's children went out they had to call home regularly. That was another item on Tsippi's list of terrorism Do's: *Take a phone, stay in touch.*

The two mothers tried to meet but each time they set a date, a bomb or a killing made it too dangerous to cross the border. So we stepped in and finally they met on the Mount of Olives, on the walkway with its magnificent view across the sloping Garden of Gethsemane to the minarets and church spires inside the ancient walls of the Holy City. First they hugged silently, then each kissed the other on the cheek, smiling shyly.

*Najwa and Idit*

"How are you?" Najwa asked, pulling back to size up Idit.

"I'm OK, how are you?" Idit answered.

"I'm fine."

"You look beautiful."

"You too."

"Are you nervous?" Idit asked.

"I was. Now I'm not anymore."

We left the Israeli and the Palestinian to talk alone for half an hour, until they hugged again, parted and returned to their very different lives, now leavened with compassion and understanding.

Later Najwa's conclusion was that there can be peace. "But peace needs a lot of time, peace needs the world to understand."

They parted as friends, with some hope for the future. But there would be no fairy-tale ending. The suicide bombs worsened, and Idit lived in fear, while Israeli soldiers imposed monthlong curfews on Palestinian towns that drove Najwa and her children to bored desperation. Over six months the friendship between the two mothers faded until they stopped communicating altogether. When we spoke to Najwa again she said she was experiencing anger like she had never experienced before, while Idit summed up her feelings in four succinct words: "Hope seems ridiculous now."

———————————

The apparently endless conflict between Israel and the Palestinians is usually framed as Jews and Arabs fighting over one piece of land. But as the story of Najwa and Idit shows, I think it's better seen as a war between those who seek peace and those who seek war. Because polls routinely show that plenty of Israelis, and plenty of Palestinians, certainly a majority on both sides, would sign a peace treaty tomorrow if it were on the table. They've had enough of fighting and want a peaceful future for their children. Instead, each side is held hostage by uncompromising leaders and fanatical ideologues.

I learned this simple truth from a remarkable woman, Nurit Peled-Elhanan, a professor of language and education at the Hebrew University of Jerusalem. A leading, and divisive, leftist figure in Israel and fighter for Palestinian rights, the European Parliament awarded her its 2001 Sakharov Prize for Human Rights and Freedom of Speech. Her grandfather had signed

Israel's Declaration of Independence. Her father, an army major general, had fought for equal rights and Nurit taught her own four children to strive for peace.

Then as the sun beat down in Jerusalem's Ben Yehuda pedestrian street, Nurit's thirteen-year-old daughter Smadar was strolling with friends, enjoying ice creams, when two suicide bombers blew themselves up among the crowd of Jews. They killed fourteen people and wounded a hundred and eighty-eight. Smadar escaped the first blast, dropped her ice cream and fled into the arms of the second Palestinian terrorist who blew himself up with Smadar in his grip.

Did the slaughter of her daughter shake Nurit's faith in the possibility of peace? No. It was reaffirmed. As her family tried to process the unspeakable tragedy that had befallen them, and condolences poured in from Israelis and Palestinians, someone asked her how she could accept words of grief from the enemy. She answered that she hadn't. Nurit explained that for her, the enemy is not the Palestinian people, it's anybody of any faith who seeks war, not peace. Her sisters, she said, are bereaved mothers, whether Jews in Israel or Arabs in the West Bank and Gaza. She insisted that we suffer with each other, not against each other. It was a remarkable testimony of faith from a woman whose only daughter had just been murdered.

And when asked about revenge, Nurit said simply, "What's the point?" And she quoted the Jewish poet Bialik: "Satan has not yet devised a vengeance for the death of a young child."

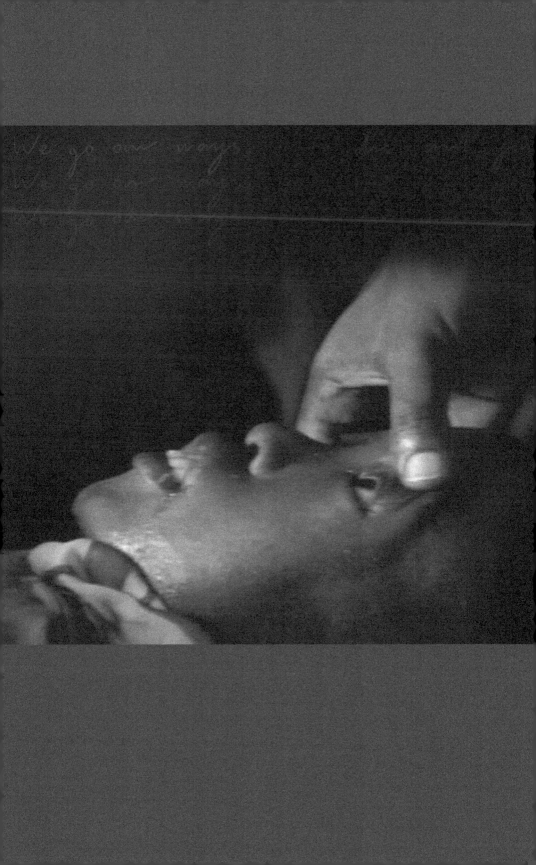

## SOMALIA 1994

*Fida Ibrahim's chest became still. Sister Annette leaned forward and gently closed her eyes. Her father had no tears left. In three weeks Mohammed had buried his wife and four other children, dead from starvation. Mounds of stones marked his journey.*

# Fida Ibrahim

WE CALL IT SOPHIE'S CHOICE, the need to make an unbearable moral decision, such as which child to save and which to abandon. The quandary seems unfathomable. And yet in almost every tiny shelter I passed, and there were hundreds of them, assembled from branches, twigs and plastic, a parent faced that very dilemma—which child to feed, which to let starve to death.

It was a time of war, drought and famine. When the first light glinted on the plastic sheeting, aid workers trod from hut to hut, peering inside, searching for the child at the back, in the murky recess, the one which the parents had judged would not survive and so was not worth feeding. They were all hungry, many were sick and dying, so better to give the little food there was to the ones that had a chance to live.

In the gloom we found Fida Ibrahim, a dying bag of skin and bones. Aid workers pulled her from the hovel and loaded her onto a broken wooden wheelbarrow, arms and legs flopping over the sides, and they pushed her, moaning in pain, through the mud and past the blank faces of the refugees to the clinic at the entrance to the feeding station in the center of Mogadishu.

Fida was suffering from scabies, a worm under the skin that spreads; malaria, that attacks the brain and lungs; and tuberculosis, which presses painfully on the internal organs. Her limbs were like matchsticks and her only chance to live was an intravenous drip, antibiotics and care in the makeshift clinic.

There, volunteers maneuvered Fida through the narrow door and laid her on a blanket on the concrete floor. Refilling the saline solution in the IV drip, the Irish nun said, "Where there's life, there's hope, that's what we say in Somalia today."

She spooned water between Fida's lips, but Fida was too far gone and after four hours her chest stopped its barely discernible rising and falling. It was still. It was over. She was twenty years old. With a sigh her father, Mohammed, crouching at her side, allowed a nurse to close her eyes. He had no tears left. On the hundred and twenty-mile trek from the town of Baidoa to the feeding station in the capital, three weeks of torment, he had buried his wife and four other children. Mounds of stones marked their journey.

Allahu Akhbar. God is great, they intoned quietly at Fida's grave, a dirge-like murmur, as they wrapped her corpse in a white sheet and lowered her into the ground.

Then, lunch. Rice and beans. Mohammed's four remaining children sat with him, their eyes bright, their skin taut, their hair thick and knotted.

Mohammed's choice.

All he prayed for now was an end to the war that had caused the famine, and for rain to end the drought. All he wanted, he said, was to go home, plant his crops, raise his cattle, find a new wife, and sit under the tree.

It was that last wish that stayed with me, that seemed to me greater than the sum of its parts. Who doesn't want to sit in the shade of a tree on a sunny day, drink in hand, listening to music or reading a good book, watching the children run and jump, with a loved one rocking on a wooden swing?

Mohammed would settle for less: maize to sow, a goat to milk, and a wife for comfort. Yet it wasn't his God who would end the war, but the Somali warlords, and they were making too much money from the famine to end their feuds.

The strongest and most ruthless warlord was Mohammed Farrah Aidid, stony-faced, cold-eyed, educated in Rome and Moscow, a man of immense experience: onetime Italian police-man, army general, Somali ambassador to India, imprisoned for six years, clan leader, and by the time I was his house guest, a master manipulator. Aidid was getting rich on the famine, and the longer it lasted, the richer he got. His men demanded ten percent of all food aid donated by international agencies. His men then looted the warehouses, while more of his men demanded protection money to stop the looters. His men both guarded the roads and attacked vehicles on the roads, all while fighting off the rival warlord, Ali Mahdi, who controlled north-ern Mogadishu, while Aidid ran the south. They all welded anti-aircraft guns and machine guns onto the back of Toyota pickups and used them as attack vehicles, homemade armored personnel carriers, which they dubbed 'technicals.'

It was in one of these that our bodyguards, assigned by Aidid, and high on the local drug khat, ferried us from the ramshackle airport to our safe house, which had earlier housed the CIA. From there we reported on the war and the famine. Later, after we had left, Aidid's men killed two dozen Pakistani UN soldiers, making him the world's most wanted man, and prompting America to send in its elite fighters to find him.

They didn't, but my NBC news team did, and, barefoot in his safe house, he warned us that the American intervention would end badly for America, which it did, in an epic way. His men killed eighteen US special forces soldiers and seriously wounded seventy more, while losing a thousand dead of their own. The ferocious battle was painfully recounted in Mark Bowden's excellent book, *Black Hawk Down*, and led to America's ignominious withdrawal from Somalia.

But this is not to tell war stories. The point is that although there was plenty of food stored in the port of Mogadishu, enough to feed a million people for a month, the food could not be handed to the hungry. The larger aid agencies, as well as the United Nations, reluctant to bow to warlord blackmail, delayed distribution until they could prevent, or at least reduce, the thieving and corruption. When UN troops finally broke the grip of the warlords, by guarding the food convoys with jeeps and helicopters, food finally started flowing in larger quantities, and the famine gradually loosened. But too late for Mohammed Ibrahim, who buried his fifth child, Fida, and prayed for peace.

---

It was a similar story during the famine in Sudan a few years earlier. There, too, tens of thousands died of starvation, while locally grown grain overflowed in the cavernous warehouses of the capital Khartoum. The government wouldn't release the food to its people. Why? The most vicious of vicious circles. Sudan wouldn't feed its hungry because it needed to sell its grain harvest overseas to earn foreign exchange to buy foreign guns and ammunition to fight its civil war at home, which was what had helped to cause the famine in the first place, and then to prolong it.

The government did allow foreign food aid to help the starving, and coming in it passed through the same port as the local grain going out. The foreign food was a gift from the concerned world, to be distributed free to the needy. But there was a catch. Yes, the grain itself was free. But to get it, families first had to pay the Sudanese government the equivalent of seventy American cents for transport, and thirty cents for tax. Each donation of two small cans of grain, about four pounds in weight, enough to feed four people for a week, cost one American dollar. And if you didn't have the money, you didn't get the food. That was the final insult and the kiss of death for many, especially infants.

Months earlier, after the last of their animals had been killed for food, which for us would mean emptying our bank account of the last penny, the desert tribespeople had no alternative but to trek to the capital in search of food and water. Tens of thousands came from all directions, squatting on the edge of town, so many and so close to the city center that the government was embarrassed and furious at this public proof of its failed policies. How could there not be enough water in the capital, built at the confluence of the Blue and White Niles? The government's response was not to release the stocks of grain and feed its people but the opposite; it stopped feeding the hungry, telling them government trucks would take them back to their abandoned villages where they would find fresh supplies of food and water.

We had gotten to know one of the refugees, Mohammed Farha and his family of seven, so now we wanted to follow them to their village a hundred and twenty miles into the Sahara desert to see the truth. Would there be food? Would there be water? Medicine for the sick infants?

But we missed their departure in a government truck, the only time anything ever happened early rather than late, so in two jeeps we set off in pursuit. But night fell and we quickly got lost in the desert. Our two guides bickered, swore it was this way. No, that way. We were lost in the barren vastness, dunes gently shifting in the breeze, any track long since erased. By now it was two o'clock in the morning, freezing cold with a sliver of moon casting just enough light to make out our anxious eyes. We drove in ever-decreasing circles until we came to a halt, sand approaching the axles, hopelessly disoriented in the icy night. "Do we know the way back to Khartoum?" I asked tentatively. While the guides pointed in different directions and argued, I tried forlornly to get a signal on our satellite phone, the cameraman slept, oblivious, and the sound man claimed to identify every constellation in the sky. Then our producer, Bert Medley, a Philly native, suddenly pronounced: "The village is that way!" He pointed into the darkness, across the unforgiving desert. The guides stopped fighting and I gave up on the phone.

"How do you know?" I said.

"I checked on the stars when we set off," Bert answered, pointing into the sky, "and I can see how they're aligned, so

*Feeding station*

that's the direction we were going and that," he said pointing into the dark, "is the way we have to drive."

Nobody had a better idea, so off we went. And blow me down, three hours later we drove straight into the village. It was a marvel of survival from a man who had brought three cases of toilet paper to begin his assignment in Israel because he had heard the paper there was rough.

Mohammed greeted us with surprise and the joyful news that food would soon be distributed. Before setting out he had told us that he didn't believe the government officials but had no choice. The promise of food at home was better than the certainty of no food in the capital. And there was, indeed, a pile of sacks of grain, with officials carefully measuring each family's supply in a tin can.

But Mohammed's relief didn't last long. Remember that catch? No money, no food? He didn't have a dollar.

Of course we gave him the money, and a good deal more, so Mohammed was set for years.

But here's another thing we often cannot truly grasp: how rare a gift it is to always to have what we need, even if it's just the minimum. Ten percent of the world's population lives on less than two dollars a day; that's less than it costs to feed a cow in Europe. In that world, a dollar means a lot.

One day while waiting for a ferry to cross a river in Tanzania, I went to buy a bag of peanuts. There was a muddy river bank, the top lined by a row of shacks selling vegetables, fruit, leaves and herbs. I had a thousand-shilling note, and the peanuts cost fifty. The peanut seller looked at the note and waved it away. He gestured to his money pouch and I understood: not enough change. I looked around, waving my bill. "Does anyone have change for a thousand shillings?" I called out in English. Blank stares from the shopkeepers. My guide shouted the same in Swahili. Shrugs all round. It was a busy market and people were bustling and pushing, a man glared impatiently at me and a stout woman in a red wraparound shawl squeezed between us.

The ferry, a flat wooden pontoon, was just heaving into sight, propelled by men with long oars, and I was stuck. I wanted the bag of peanuts and nobody could break a thousand-shilling note, the equivalent of a one-dollar bill. The entire commerce was conducted in single digits. No wonder the peanut vendor's jaw fell in disbelief when I walked away with twenty bags, and the children on the pontoon could not believe their luck when I gave away nineteen.

## RWANDA 1994

*Machete \ma-she-te\ n : a large heavy knife used to cut sugarcane and underbrush and as a weapon.* Merriam-Webster Dictionary.

*And as a weapon. However low-tech, the Hutus slaughtered the Tutsis at a faster rate than the Nazis killed Jews, with nothing but machetes and clubs. Rivers filled with corpses and blood, in a country where they say: Nobody hates himself more than he who hates others.*

TEACHER SEVEN

# *Emmanuel*

THERE WERE TWO EMMANUELS, the killer and the victim. A Hutu
and a Tutsi. The two men with the shared name were wheeling
their bicycles along a dusty track and chatting when I came across
them near the genocide memorial in Ntamara, a church about
twenty miles from Rwanda's capital, Kigali. They represented, or
so it seemed, a lesson in forgiveness, for that is one of the many
lessons that emerged from the Rwandan genocide in 1994, when
Hutus went on their murderous rampage. In a hundred days they
slaughtered eight hundred thousand Tutsis, mostly by smashing
their skulls with clubs and machetes. The Hutus tossed thousands
of corpses into the Kagera River. They drifted and bobbed with the
current, plunged over waterfalls, and ultimately the bodies were
dumped into resplendent Lake Victoria, a hundred and twenty
miles away.

The Hutu Emmanuel was shorter, squatter. Eyes downcast, tone
resigned, he spoke in terse but stony statements of fact. "I cut them.
Yeah. I used the machete. Here," he said, drawing his finger across
his throat, "and there," indicating his lower back. "I killed them."

"Them" were a woman and her daughter, cousins of the other Emmanuel, the Tutsi. This Emmanuel was taller, leaner, clean-shaven and clean-cut, standing straight and proud.

Copying the Truth and Reconciliation Commission that tried to heal the rift between black and white citizens of South Africa after the collapse of apartheid, Rwanda set up a similar mechanism after the genocide. And it seemed to work. As long as the Hutu killer admitted guilt and apologized, he could be redeemed by society, his prison time could be reduced and he could be forgiven by his Tutsi neighbors. It worked for the two Emmanuels. "I must accept and forgive," the Tutsi victim said.

But back when I was reporting on the Rwandan genocide I marveled at how shallow was this so-called tribal difference that led to such mass murder. Reporting on and living with apartheid in Southern Africa, as I had for four years, was simpler; not to belabor the point, it was more black and white. But the difference between Hutu and Tutsi, not so much. In fact, it was hard to establish any difference between them at all.

True, the two Emmanuels embodied the physical stereotypes. Hutus are said to be shorter and squatter with more pronounced so-called African features, like a squatter nose and thicker lips. Tutsis are said to be taller, leaner, have a thinner nose and higher cheekbones. The Emmanuels could have been straight out of central casting's Stereotypes Handbook.

But the reality of the Hutu/Tutsi difference, that engendered such murderous ferocity, is so minor as to be indiscernible. Frankly, it is a lesson on how stupid it is to demonize the so-called "other."

So what is the "otherness" that led to genocide?

It is believed that about three thousand years ago, tribesmen trekked from the south to this region of central Africa and settled, planting crops and living off the land. Around two thousand years later, other tribesmen came from the north and mostly raised cattle. They mixed with the first lot, and adopted their language and traditions, even their religious beliefs. But because raising cattle earned more money than raising crops, the new arrivals tended to be wealthier.

That was the only difference, until the Europeans arrived. In the 1880s, along came the Belgian colonists who introduced identity cards for so-called Hutus and Tutsis and favored the wealthier cattle raisers. They educated the Tutsi young in Belgium and trained them to lord over the poorer and less fortunate vegetable growers. That was the colonial way. Divide and rule.

Tribal difference? No. It was about money and privilege, and the differences hardened into artificial tribal labels, which inevitably provoked rivalry and made the conflict easier to understand—more black and white.

We have the phrase, "It's the economy, Stupid." There, the phrase was, "It's the labels, Stupid," which had one upside. While the Hutu/Tutsi labels divided the people, when the genocidal dust settled, the absence of real substance made it easier to overcome the prejudice of the recent past, and for the Truth and Reconciliation process to take hold.

Today it is considered impolite to use the labels Hutu or Tutsi. "We are all Rwandans now" is the official line on the thirteen million citizens. One former Tutsi soldier told us, "Today we have one ID, one language, we are one people." But only time will judge whether the victims and the killers have truly buried the machetes. Still, in a world of vendettas, feuds and vicious power struggles, it's a relief to know that even in the most deadly of places, there can be a willingness, and a way, to find peace, however passing. That's another way of saying, never give up.

It was a good conversation, that bore out the government's mission to heal the wounds and end the enmity. When we said our farewells, the two Emmanuels, killer and victim, turned as one and waved to us. They wheeled their bikes away, with nary a glance at the church that held ten thousand battered skulls.

———————————

Back in Kigali, government officials were discussing the planning of a national memorial to the genocide, larger and more imposing than the six different church memorials that had been built around the country. I mentioned Israel's Holocaust memorial in Jerusalem, a moving monument to the murder of six million Jews by the Germans and their European puppets. I described the crescendo of emotions engendered by the rooms full of relics and testimonies and the great release provided by the end of the exhibit, when the corridor opens onto a wide vista of the Jerusalem hills awash in cypress trees and bougain-villea. A wave of relief at the simple beauty of the landscape washes over the visitor after the horrors of the exhibition. The ending provides nature's cleansing and it is a stroke of genius by the planners.

*Ntamara Memorial - Photo by Paul Goldman*

And in fact, Israel did help the Rwandans plan their capital's genocide memorial, a grim contribution from a dreadful
shared memory. The big difference is that whereas Jerusalem's
Holocaust memorial is composed of relics and images and
recorded statements of survivors, Rwanda's is more brutally
overt. It is housed in a squat, concrete building on a hill on the
edge of Kigali, atop the skeletons and skulls of two hundred and
fifty thousand Tutsis.

KENYA 2008

*They look healthy and curious, these Maasai boys, yet they suffer from the curse of Africa. A traditional blessing for the Maasai newborn is, "May you stay healthy in drought and in rain," because the water they drink is so dirty it can kill.*

# Four Maasai Boys

MISOGYNIST ALERT!

It is changing slowly, as education spreads, but there still exists a world where a man buys his wife with cows, marries as many women as he likes and shares them with his friends, who in turn share their wives.

The wives milk the cows, walk miles to fetch and carry water, walk more miles to collect and carry wood, feed and raise the children, wash clothes in the river, and build huts with cow dung and urine. When a man wants, he can divorce his wife as long as the other men of the tribe agree. But a woman cannot divorce a man.

This is the world of the Maasai, striking semi-nomads, tourist magnets, who live along the Great Rift Valley of East Africa.

I asked one Maasai man, Ben, what he did all day while the women worked. "I work too," he answered, taking offense. "What do you think I do? I herd the cattle. I take them out in the morning and bring them back at night."

Maasai men are tall, lithe and swift. They walk for many hours at great speed. I peered across the savannah into the distant hills of the escarpment, shielding my eyes from the blinding sun, searching for his cattle. The Maasai measure their wealth in cows, and herding them was a great responsibility. "Where are they?" I asked. Maybe they were so far away I couldn't even see them.

"There," Ben said, pointing in the opposite direction. I turned. And there were his cattle, lolling and grazing by the nearest tree, a hundred yards away.

"That's your day?" I asked.

"Today, yes. But sometimes I rest."

Wow, I thought, these guys must live forever. But in fact, the average life expectancy of the Maasai male is possibly the lowest in the world. They die on average at the age of forty-two, and their women outlive them by only two years.

Their diet may be part of the reason: maize, maize, maize and large amounts of meat, milk, and blood, harvested from their valuable cattle. The water they drink comes from streams and springs they share with their cattle and wild animals. Diseases like typhoid and dysentery are a fact of life.

I met Patrick in a noisy clinic in the Maasai Mara National Park. The room was crowded with mothers who had walked for many miles, cradling their sick babies, to that last resort, the man in the white coat. The babies were wrapped in blankets, fast asleep or wailing in pain. They suffered from the same symptoms as Patrick, who was twelve years old: fever, diarrhea, stomach cramps, vomiting and sweating. The verdict was the same for all of them: typhoid, caused by either drinking dirty water or playing on the ground in mud—earth mixed with infected water.

Patrick had suffered from one waterborne disease or another every year of his life, his father James said, but it wasn't always like this. Once his entire Maasai boma, or village, drank water from the same spring and nobody ever fell sick. "So what's changed?" I asked.

"Too many people today, too many animals, the water gets dirty," he answered. Population growth and increased herd sizes compete for declining amounts of water; much of the available water is used for agriculture, which is expanding.

It's hard to imagine that of Africa's 1.2 billion people, almost one in three has no access to clean water. And no Perrier for Patrick, no San Pellegrino. Some do suck water through filters that eliminate most of the bacteria, like the LifeStraws shown on this book's cover, but they are a drop in the bucket, so to speak. Even in the capital Nairobi, people fall sick from the water.

Hospitals don't always help. When we were there the national newspaper carried a story headed: "Skeleton Found in Hospital Tank." In Nandi South District, the paper reported, hospital patients and staff had been drinking from a water tank with a decomposing body inside. Patients found human hair in their cups. They all gathered to watch as the skeleton was pulled out.

Small wonder that a Maasai blessing for a new-born is: "May you stay healthy in rain and in drought."

But it's a mixed blessing for the children I met who were as curious about me as I was about them. Their culture and traditions attract foreign tourists who come for the dramatic wildlife in the Maasai Mara and Serengeti National Parks, together the size of Hawaii, then take side trips to visit the colorful tribe that lives in harmony with the animals. They listen to the Maasai sing, they enjoy their dances and watch the men bound straight-legged into the air from a standing position in a form of mating dance. Tourists buy eye-catching beaded jewelry that the Maasai wear around their necks and hang from their ears. Guides recount dramatic tales of bygone years when young men went alone into the bush and learned to hunt lions with spears, and they relate how in their lifetimes the boys grow from junior warriors to senior warriors, to junior elders and then senior elders, when it becomes their turn to make decisions for the tribe. The rhythm of their lives is as set as the seasons.

"But what about the girls?" I asked. Not such a selling point. The guides avoid the taboo issue of forced circumcision—of how girls are cut before marriage, a Maasai rite of passage from childhood to adulthood, in which all or part of the clitoris, and at times the adjacent labia, are removed. The painful and cruel procedure is illegal today, which just means it is carried out earlier, when the girls are as young as eleven, so that it can be done before the nosy inspectors come looking.

So yes, I learned a lot from Maasai traditions, mostly about what not to do. In a more trivial example, under the rubric of How Not to Treat a Guest, the warriors, who had been lounging around under the tree all morning, roasted a goat, which smelled delicious, and although I'm no meat eater, I was salivating, as were my teammates from NBC News. With their hunting daggers the men carved the flesh into roasted chunks and distributed them. To each other. "Uh, hello, what about us?" I ventured.

Your guests? It turned out that because we were men without daggers, and so not real men, we couldn't eat the meat.

Anyway, I asked, unwrapping my last granola bar, what were they doing lounging under the tree all day long, armed with spears and daggers? Protecting the village from attack? Yes, I was told, exactly. But nobody could remember the last time an enemy had appeared.

When Kipas, the village elder, presented me with a gift of a talking stick, which I'll explain in a moment, I humbly accepted it with my left hand, as I was holding a camera in the right. He snatched it back in alarm. "Never with the left hand!"

"Oh, sorry," I said.

"It is our custom," he explained.

Much here is excused in the name of tradition and custom, but the talking stick was one custom that I embraced.

It always bugs me how often people interrupt each other. In conversations many barely listen, rather we wait for an opportunity to interject. It is rare to complete a thought. So when Kipas explained the talking stick, I was thrilled.

When the council of men gathers, whoever holds the talking stick, speaks. Everyone else listens. If you want to talk, you wait until you are handed the talking stick, so that conversation can be calm, dignified and productive. The stick is a narrow piece of smoothed wood about eighteen inches long with a knob on one end, like a small club, decorated with brightly colored, patterned beads. It is a thing of honor and I was charmed by the gift.

Goading him only somewhat, I asked if women have talking sticks too. Kipas' smile faded. He gave me a withering look.

The irritated tone of his response, the most drawn-out syllable I have ever heard, contained all the frustration of an ancient, proud tribe of semi-nomadic men struggling to fend off the encroachment of a modern era.

"Uh. No-oooo."

Yet here's the odd thing. In the days that I spent with the Maasai, the dominant sound in the boma and around the water spring and in the fields was of women laughing. They chattered cheerfully with each other as they washed their clothes in the water and stroked the heads of their children as they fed them. They sang as they walked through the fields with impossibly heavy loads balanced on their heads. As they toiled and bore the burdens of life in a Maasai boma, one word came to mind—acceptance. They accepted their lot, seemed to embrace it even, and I admired their strength and endurance.

That was my first thought, anyway, until it hit me that my rosy first impression might merely be channelling a smug plantation owner in the southern states of America, circa 1850. "I have the happiest slaves in America," he may have said, describing for his New York friends how his black slaves danced and crooned in the cotton fields back home.

And here, I thought, as I watched the women laboring and singing, was a different form of abuse and oppression: not of blacks by whites, but of women by men. Like the slaves in America, the women here also had little option but acceptance, no way to rebel against their exploitation. James, my Maasai guide, for instance, had three wives, each of whom he had married when she was fifteen. Together they had twenty-one children.

But with the spread of schools and education, with the

*Maasai women in Kipas' village*

appearance of female teachers and nurses, Maasai girls now have a few role models who are inspiring change. Some of the girls no longer accept being one of multiple wives. Birth control means smaller families, which gives women more time for themselves. Some have begun small businesses like selling milk or making honey that they sell through women's cooperatives.

Change is slow, however. Men meeting under the tree still decide everything, and the further the people live from town, the more entrenched are the old ways.

So my most lasting response to the tourist phenomenon that are the Maasai tribespeople, with their lithe beauty, with their adornments of colorful beads, living so close to nature, at one with their cattle and earth, was this: I really would not like to be a Maasai woman.

ISRAEL/WEST BANK 2004

"If music be the food of love, play on," *wrote William Shakespeare in* Twelfth Night. *But if it's the sound of oppression it may strike a different note. Play, the soldier ordered the violin student, or you can't pass. And the cry rose in Israel: What have we come to?*

# *Wissam Tayem*

HE HAD ONLY PLAYED THE VIOLIN for six weeks, a Chinese knockoff that cost him six hundred shekels, about a hundred and fifty dollars. So when the soldier told him to play something, Wissam Tayem didn't have much of a repertoire. But he did manage a couple of tunes that he played over and over.

It was his first time playing in public, and he was nervous. Not because of the audience—there wasn't one—but because of the soldiers with the guns. It was an Israeli army roadblock and Wissam said that the soldier told him to play something sad while he checked his papers to see if he would be allowed to pass through.

And so the Palestinian played the violin at the order of the Israeli soldiers, and one witness, a Jewish woman, Horit Peled, was beyond shocked. "It was the association with the Holocaust," she said after filming the incident. Everybody understood: the Nazis had forced Jews to play music while other Jews died. A musical accompaniment to mass murder.

Was the comparison overwrought?

Many didn't think so. The soldier and the violinist sparked a debate among shocked Israelis who wondered, What have we come to? Is this why we came to this dry land, to behave like those who abused and destroyed us? Have we become the abusers?

Others said, Slow down. The soldier was just doing his job. Military sources told one reporter that the Palestinian may have been carrying explosives in his violin and that the soldier had been correct to check.

The argument raged across the land, or at least among opinion columnists sensing a story with legs. How can you compare a soldier who forced a man to play the violin with Nazis who murdered six million of us? An insensitive soldier at a border crossing was a far cry from a homicidal maniac in a concentration camp. Or was it rather, some asked, one more step down the path of racist oppression? The confrontation between the soldier and the violinist became the latest flare-up in the perpetual debate among Israelis, born of anxiety and insecurity, about what kind of country the Jewish state is, and should be.

But nobody was more surprised by the furor than the violinist himself. He was besieged by reporters seizing the opportunity to go for Israel's jugular, while all Wissam had worried about was being late for his violin class. After a few minutes he had been allowed to pass. He quickly dismissed the incident saying, "What do you expect, that's what Israelis are like."

And then another, more welcome, surprise. Sympathetic Israeli musicians at a violin workshop invited Wissam to join them. He was delighted. And so a few days later, the Palestinian music student, in a new grey suit and matching tie, passed smoothly through the same roadblock on the way to kibbutz Eilon in Israel's western Galilee to participate in a three-day seminar for violinists. "I came here because I wanted to study music and to become a professional violinist, not because of politics," he told reporters. "But if my violin serves as another bridge to peace, then naturally I don't object."

Others did object, however, notably those Palestinians who believe any form of normalcy with Israel is a sellout of the Palestinian cause because it validates their oppression. Getting to know the enemy is treachery.

One of the first Israelis Wissam got to know at the seminar was the master violin maker and restorer, Amnon Weinstein, who tweaked and plucked, turned pegs and tightened strings, sweetening the notes from Wissam's mass-produced Chinese model. Wissam looked on in awe. It turned out Weinstein was the right man for the job, for more than one reason. His knowledge went way beyond tuning this beginner's instrument. By a remarkable twist, Weinstein knew a thing or two about explosives in violins.

Weinstein often recounted the tale of a wrecked violin he had restored after it had been found cracked and molding in a damp attic in Ukraine where it had lain for decades. A twelve-year-old violinist called Yossele, working with the anti-Nazi resistance in the Second World War, had used his violin-playing gig in a Nazi officers club to smuggle in explosives he had hidden in his violin case. A resistance fighter had then assembled the bomb and had succeeded in blowing up the Nazi club, killing and wounding two hundred. The Nazis later caught Yossele and killed him.

Decades later, Weinstein restored Yossele's violin and the virtuoso Shlomo Mintz, in a fitting irony, played the very same violin, alone in a field in Auschwitz. It was a form of musical revenge. And now here was Weinstein, fixing up Wissam's violin, after an Israeli allegedly suspected it had contained explosives. So maybe the soldier's concern wasn't so far-fetched, especially at a time when Palestinians were seeking all kinds of original ways to smuggle bombs into Israel.

But all this went over the head of Wissam Tayem, who had never been to Israel before, and who couldn't believe his luck. Now for the first time he saw Israelis not with guns in their hands but violins, waving bows, not rifles. Not soldiers barking orders but the gentle tones of music lovers. One tutor was tactful: "Wissam has done very well but he needs to develop his ability as a violinist."

After three days of intensive instruction, Wissam hadn't improved enough to take part in the final concert, but nobody's gaze was as fixed as his as he listened from the second row, looking up with admiration at the line of violinists, so accomplished and with such flair. A hint of a smile, almost smug, played on his lips. This is my dream, he said later, and I am learning. Not only to play the violin but that peace is possible, with new friends like these.

———————————

Getting to know the enemy, through music or sport or however, is the kiss of death for conflict. That's why enemy groups dehumanize the other side and rationalize the conflict by deceiving

*Wissam Tayem*

their own people about the foe. Think, for example, of Russia's
attack on the "Nazis" of Ukraine.

In this vein Palestinian Islamic extremists routinely refer to
Jews as dogs and monkeys. Israeli Jewish extremists routinely
refer to Palestinians as terrorists and murderers. In the middle
are the majority, who speak with a softer voice, who don't deal
in facile labels, a fair number of whom are involved in organizations working for understanding and peace.

There is one such group of Israelis and Palestinians that
nobody wants to join, especially not its members. They come
together on Israel's Independence Day, which marks Israel's
War of Independence in 1948, and which Palestinians call
the Naqba, the Catastrophe. Each side commemorates the

event in its own nationalist manner. The Israelis party and the Palestinians mourn. But this one group of reluctant members observes in its own alternative way, a more inclusive way.

It is pain that brings them together, for these are Israelis and Palestinians who share a common grief: the death of a loved one.

It could be a son in Israeli uniform killed by Palestinian fighters or a daughter blown up by a suicide bomber. It could be the parents of the bomber or a boy shot in the throat by an Israeli soldier. They mourn together. They share grief but not hatred. Pain but not lust for revenge.

They want peace, like the Palestinian parents of Ahmed Khatib.

Ahmed was twelve years old, playing with a toy gun in the West Bank town of Jenin, when a bullet tore through his throat. Israeli soldiers fighting nearby had apparently mistaken him for an enemy fighter. He was rushed to Rambam, the Israeli hospital in Haifa. It took two days for him to die, and during that traumatic time his father saw other children fighting for their lives. It tore at his heart to see their families' pain. So when Ahmed lost the struggle, his father Ismail and his mother, Abla, donated his organs. Describing that day a decade and a half earlier, Ismail told the alternative gathering on Independence Day, 2022: "It was one of the hardest decisions I have ever had to make, my humanity drove me to agree." He gave his son's heart, liver, lungs, kidneys and more. Abla said, "My son has died, God rest his soul. Maybe he can give life to others."

The donation by an Arab family was seen by many as a peace overture that could break the ice. For five of the six recipients were Jews.

Ehud Olmert, Israel's Prime Minister at the time, November 2005, called the family to apologize. The Palestinian leader, Mahmoud Abbas, thanked them. Even a local Palestinian militia leader, Zakaria Zubeideh, saw good in the donation. "I don't think an Israeli with a Palestinian organ will now kill a Palestinian," he said.

Thanks to the gesture of his parents, Ahmed's death led to a rare chink in the armor of hatred, a glimpse of an alternative to bullets and bombs. But it didn't last long. For societies are ruled more by fear than by faith, more by envy than by goodwill, and while one individual's generosity may inspire the few, it won't change the minds of the many.

To be fair, Jesus accomplished that change. So did Mahatma Gandhi and Nelson Mandela, and no doubt a good many more unsung heroes. But Israelis and Palestinians? They are still waiting for their Messiahs.

LAPITHOS, CYPRUS - JUNE 1974 - PAUL RO

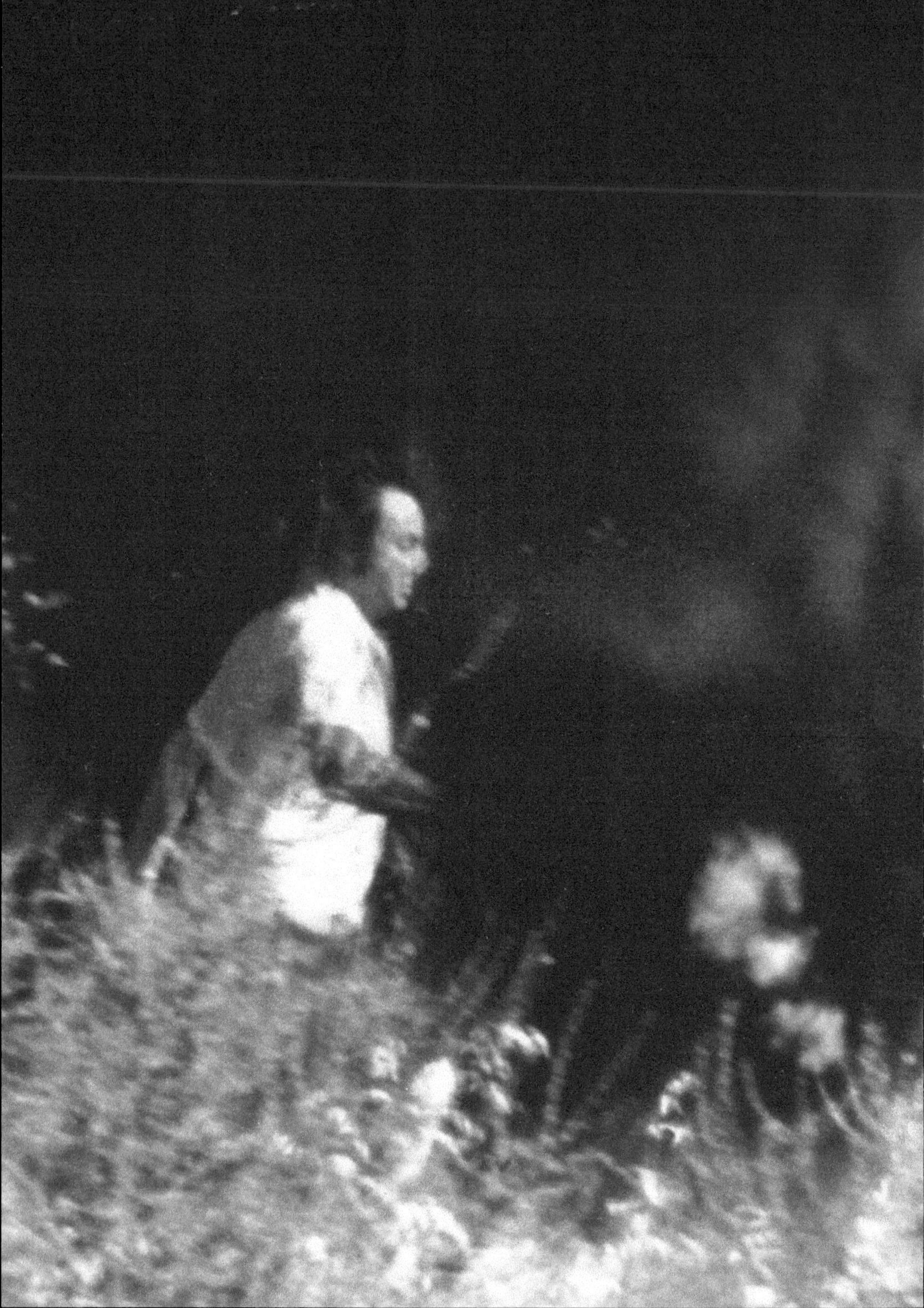

STEPS ON AP MINE

CYPRUS, 1974

*Ted lay dead in the
minefield and Simon lay
wounded. Paul went to
help. But he didn't see the
land mine, death in the
ground, and that should
have been the end of him.*

# Paul and Neil

PAUL ROQUE WENT TO HELP SIMON DRING, who had tried to help Ted Stoddart, who had tried to help everyone by warning them of the unmarked minefield. The sequence of good intentions left Ted dead, Paul seriously wounded, and Simon bleeding out on the ground.

Moments earlier, Ted, a BBC soundman and father of three, had trod on a Bouncing Betty which exploded at chest height and pierced his heart. Simon, the BBC correspondent, was ripped by shrapnel from yet another explosion. To avoid the lethal land mines, Paul, an Associated Press photographer, had stepped off the dirt stretch and into the brush lining the road. He didn't know that more mines were buried in the grass.

The Turkish army had turned an innocuous rural road into a death trap to prevent Greek tanks and troops from approaching their positions near Lapithos, a strategic village which spreads prettily up the foot of the Kyrenia mountains, overlooking the coastal plain of Cyprus. We had wanted to see if villagers had returned to their homes after the Turks invaded the island. With hindsight, it was of little interest beyond journalists looking for a good story on a quiet news day.

It was nine o'clock in the morning when Paul, striding quickly and looking at me, and then ahead, instead of the ground, landed with his full weight on the pressure-triggered anti-personnel mine. There was a sharp crack, an explosion of black smoke and flames that swallowed him, a whoosh of hot wind that took my breath away, and burning steel that sliced through the air in all directions. The mine had a kill radius of fifty feet. The blast blackened Paul's hair and skin, tore out an eye and some of his nose, and shattered his limbs. Yet, somehow, Paul staggered away, blood pouring from his wounds.

He fell into a car with another journalist whose stomach was blown open, and another whose hand was almost severed. Another car held journalists with lesser wounds. They fled. The minefield had turned a minor morning news reconnaissance into a bloodbath.

I was just plain lucky. Inch by inch I picked my way out of the minefield unscathed. Physically at least.

---

"No story is worth dying for" is the most common platitude of war reporters. Yet in every war, reporters die. It is a hard business, exceptionally dangerous, with slim rewards for most, beyond personal satisfaction. Yet it attracts the best and the brightest, for reasons incomprehensible to reasonable people. After all, why risk your life in a strange country, for people you don't know, speaking a language you don't understand, fighting a war about which you know little?

Deskbound editors at head offices have their own set of idle bromides: Keep your head down, Stay safe, Don't do anything I wouldn't do. These admonishments are as redundant as the immediate response everyone has when somebody else trips and falls: Be careful, we call out, when it is too late.

No reporter thinks they will be killed or even injured; they always think catastrophe will happen to somebody else. In the same way, no soldier thinks they will die that day, no fireman thinks he will be trapped under a burning beam, no policeman thinks he will be shot that day in a routine traffic stop. Yet all these individuals go to work knowing that there is always a chance that they will not see their home or loved ones again. So why do they do it? There are as many reasons as there are war reporters; the only thing they have in common is a mother who says, "Get another job."

To reduce risk to journalists, as well as potential legal liability to themselves, wealthier news organizations today send journalists to workshops on how to cope in war zones, known as HEFAT— Hostile Environment and First Aid Training. The course is all about anticipating danger, reducing time exposed to danger, and how to stay alive if unlucky enough to be caught in the middle of it. Former special forces fighters and ex-cops bully, browbeat and generally give journalists a hard time to prepare them for the worst, as well as instruct them in the lethal functions of weapons of all kinds, including biological and chemical. In most courses the kidnapping exercise has been discontinued for being too brutal and frightening.

Embedding is another recent way to reduce risk. It is an ugly composite word that describes a journalist being absorbed into a military unit. In the real world it means getting to know the soldiers and telling their side of the story, in return for a cot to sleep on, food and transport and an acceptable degree of risk. Basically—you scratch my back and I'll scratch yours. Although the word embed is recent, it is just another iteration of an age-old friction that pits intrepid, independent war correspondents against buttoned-down public affairs officers with a perennial agenda: Make us look good, make them look bad.

One who never submitted, who never saw the other side as bad, was Neil Davis, of Visnews and NBC News, he of the chestnut quiff, jutting jaw and quiet demeanor. He preferred the middle ground, where truth often lies.

For twenty years Neil filmed the wars in South Vietnam and Cambodia, always from the point of view of the front-line native grunt. Not for Neil the daily press conferences and American armored vehicle patrols backed by helicopters straf-ing villages. He was down and dirty, traipsing through the rice paddies with his buddies in the south Vietnamese army, and later the Cambodian, his trademark, sweat-soaked towel draped over his shoulders, film camera in hand, calming everyone in combat with his Aussie twang. He survived it all, without com-promising, without embedding, becoming a legend throughout Asia and into Africa, until one minor failed coup attempt in Thailand ended it for him. He was fifty-two years old when a tank shell hit a wall behind him and shrapnel killed Neil and his soundman, Bill Latch. His friend, Visnews cameraman Gary Burns, dragged Neil out of the line of fire, a streak of blood tracing Neil's last journey, his dropped camera recording it. Soon afterwards, Gary, shocked, resigned from his news-film agency for a less threatening and successful life in sports broadcasting.

All attempts to reduce the risk, like HEFAT courses or embedding, as well as sending ex-military types as bodyguards, another new practice, are negated by the extra lethality of modern weapons. Once upon a time, a reporter under fire could hide behind a tree or a wall until the shooting stopped. Today, one shell or rocket or even some kinds of bullet will take out the entire wall, and everyone behind it.

It makes a mockery of cliches used to describe a war reporter's life spent dodging bullets. Dodging bullets? I don't think so. You can't see them but can hear a whine, if it's close, and if it just missed you, a sudden clapping sound. The bullet was so close it displaced the air around your ear.

It is good to prepare and reduce what risks you can, but in the end, staying alive is mostly about luck. As Alan Pizzey of CBS News said, "Luck is like a blind trust fund; you can make withdrawals but not deposits, and you have no idea how much is left." Possibly the most admired and experienced combat cameraman ever, Neil's luck had ran out and so had Ted Stoddart's. Simon and Paul survived their wounds. Others escaped unscathed for entire careers. But all shared one attribute. They wanted to live life to the fullest.

"One crowded hour" was Neil's motto, and the title of a fascinating biography written by his friend Tim Bowden. Rather live one crowded hour than a life of mediocrity. At the top of every journal Neil kept was this timeless sentiment, taken from a wartime poem, "The Call," written by Thomas Osbert Mordaunt around 1760:

> "Sound, sound the clarion, fill the fife,
> Throughout the sensual world proclaim,
> One crowded hour of glorious life
> Is worth an age without a name."

I never knew what brought Neil to this fatalistic and uncompromising creed, but certainly he lived it to the full, and many followed in his wake, including me. Yet in all our free time reveling in Africa I don't believe he revealed even one intimate detail of his life. I didn't even know he was married. There was another rarely mentioned aspect to him and it may have explained why he was always bumming cigarettes. He claimed that not buying his own meant that he smoked less. Neil didn't spend much money on himself anyway. Instead, after his death we discovered that much of his income went to support orphanages for Vietnamese and Cambodian children. Neil's secret was that this tough guy had a heart of gold, and put the best face on the worst of times. After yet another near miss Neil's usually hilarious account would end with: "The situation was desperate but not serious."

Black humor was one of Neil's releases, as it is for many who daily put their lives on the line, made possible only by ill-judged trust in their own immunity. Certainly in the old days drink helped, as did sex, drugs and rock'n roll, as well as a healthy dose of self-mockery, almost a requirement for foreign correspondents. Hugh Mulligan, a fifty-year veteran of the

*Neil and Me ~ Photo by Peter Jordan*

Associated Press, nailed it with the title of his memoir: *Been Everywhere Got Nowhere.*

The lifestyle is seductive yet contradictory. A correspondent can leave home, fly first class, stay in a five-star hotel, eat in the best restaurant in town, only to arrive at a war-torn dump without power, food or clean water, then work around the clock, often risking their life.

Which part of that doesn't make sense? Or does it all make perfect sense for a certain possibly damaged personality? And is that person damaged before embarking upon such a career, or does he or she become damaged by the career? Does it take a certain type? In Africa, the joke was that you flew two thousand miles, took a train another two hundred, a car for fifty more, then an oxen for the last three miles, and when you went for a drink in the local bar, you found thirty people you knew.

Yes, it is glorious work if you can get it, but for those who routinely face combat, especially anyone who works with a camera, post-traumatic stress is a common risk factor. Some photographers and cameramen say that the viewfinder acts like a filter, distancing them from the reality, making atrocious acts unreal and therefore palatable. Others take an opposite view. While a reporter or technician can turn away from a gory sight, the people holding the cameras cannot avert their gaze. They must observe the horror in every detail, decide when to zoom in, adjust for focus and exposure, and cannot turn away. On the contrary, the cameraperson must see in sharp focus every appalling detail. No surprise then that camerapeople suffer from PTSD much more often than reporters or technicians.

But PTSD often goes unrecognized among journalists because their very presence in a combat zone is seen by some as illegitimate. At a bombing, as the dead and injured lie bleeding on the ground, some screaming for help, the medics have a clear role. So do the ambulance drivers and the policemen. But the journalists? They just get in the way. And now they're complaining of nightmares. Well guess what, goes the common response—if you don't like it, don't go. Nobody needs you there anyway.

Today that is changing and every serious news organization provides sympathy and help, beginning with the HEFAT training. The first step towards healing is to admit that there is a problem, which for many in this business is already a major concession. It wasn't always so. Take my own experience. I was never proud and made the huge mistake, many years ago, of saying that I was burned out. The response was to put me on a one-year contract instead of the usual four years, and a warning to shape up or ship out.

Today, that could not happen. Counseling and rest time have taken the place of threats, alcohol and drugs. It's a different world, fortunately, one in which it is unthinkable that one cameraman could be seriously wounded six times and lightly wounded a dozen more, as Neil Davis was. "What do you mean Neil has a death wish?" one colleague said. "He's alive, isn't he?"

But that was before he wasn't. RIP Neil, the nicest guy I ever met.

That was one hell of a crowded hour.

AUSCHWITZ, POLAND

*At least 1.3 million people entered the gates of Auschwitz. Of these, 1.1 million left as smoke through the chimney. Russian soldiers liberated seven thousand more, the sick and the dying abandoned by the SS. They were shocked by what they saw. Primo Levi recalled white carcasses dragging themselves along the ground like slugs.*

# Survivors

IN THE SUN, the cloth itched like fire ants, and in the rain, clung sodden to their skin. It hardened in the snow and ice, and itched furiously again in the thaw. The coarse material came in bolts of hundreds of meters, which prisoners sewed into the blue and grey striped uniforms of the concentration camp. Come rain or shine they reeked of sour sweat and excrement.

A badge on each uniform marked the prisoner's offense. Jews wore yellow stars, the most common in Auschwitz. Homosexuals wore pink triangles, political prisoners red triangles with a letter denoting their nationality. There were a dozen more categories of prisoners but all shared one deferred destiny: death. Deferred because they had a use—laborers, tailors, cooks, musicians, hence the uniform. A million more, especially the very young and the old, had no use and no uniforms. They were simply stripped naked and killed.

For those selected to work it was a race against time. The longer it took to die, the greater the chance to live. And so, one icy afternoon, Friday, January 27th, 1945, when the SS guards had fled, conquering Soviet soldiers, bayonets fixed, stared in disbelief at the human debris they found propping each other up behind rows of razor wire. The prisoners stared back blankly, as it sunk in that their long painful night was done. They could throw away those garments of shame. They had survived.

Today, some of those striped uniforms can be found behind glass in museums and memorials, along with piles of shoes and spectacles and hair of the six million murdered Jews. Frail nonagenarians guide schoolchildren through the gates of Auschwitz, pointing to where they slept, worked, and didn't die. Here they stood for hours in the snow, there they were beaten and hounded by dogs; in that block a thousand of them slept with rats and lice, and there they lined up for work at four-thirty in the morning.

In the history of mankind, this is the worst known crime. Yet for the young today, visiting the concentration camps is a study trip, the Holocaust has become a history class worth two credits. Indeed, a growing number say it never happened, that millions were not murdered and that the survivors are liars. Holocaust denial flourishes in Iran and the Arab world as well as in revisionist academia. In one prominent case, a British court had to adjudicate whether Jews really were gassed in Auschwitz.

As the Auschwitz inmates marched to their slave labor, the prisoner's orchestra played, in the Nazi belief that the rhythm would make it easier to control them. The most common instrument was the violin.

And so today, what better instrument to play in the killing fields of Auschwitz, in the shadows of the watchtowers, to evoke the horror of the past. Where Jews were slaughtered by the million, the virtuoso Schlomo Mintz stood alone and played a violin that survived the Holocaust, in memory of those people who did not. It was as if he summoned from the earth their suffering spirits. A witness said everybody cried and that he couldn't sleep for two months.

For me, with a family line almost extinguished in the Holocaust, the past is a bloody burden buried deep, and I am hardly alone. Early in the life of the state, when Israelis met for the first time, the icebreaker question often was: So how did your family survive the Holocaust? All had extraordinary stories, and they had to be extraordinary or they would not have survived.

My parents in London once asked me to deliver a package to a friend of theirs in Ramat Hasharon in central Israel. I couldn't decline the invitation to stay for an orange juice, so their friend and I found ourselves sitting blankly opposite each other. To be polite, I asked him where he was during the war. "In a hole in the ground," he answered.

I looked up sharply. "I beg your pardon?"

This innocuous elderly man with a brown-spotted pate and hairy ears, with kind eyes and a weary smile, who had just served me juice and chocolate chip cookies, had spent two years of his life with his sister in a freezing, damp, rat-infested hole in the ground. It was hidden by planks and a rug, on which stood the foreman's desk and chair. At night they emerged onto the empty factory floor to use the bathroom and to eat food left by the foreman who was hiding them from the Nazis. He was taking an extraordinary risk. The penalty for sheltering a Jew, giving him food or even a ride in a car, was immediate death.

Little is known about the fate of my own family. One grandfather died of a heart attack in Budapest when the Nazis came for the Jews, the other was killed in the Riga ghetto. One grandmother died of typhoid in Riga, the other's death is unknown. I can never remember their names. I have a mental block. I know nothing about the deaths of my grandparent's brothers and sisters, their aunts and uncles, their cousins or their nieces and nephews. I could maybe find out in the Holocaust archives in Jerusalem's Yad Vashem memorial, but I don't have the heart. All I know is that my mother and father survived, as did one sister of each and a niece of my father. They lived because they managed to leave Austria before the war began in September, 1939.

I have always been surprised that not one of my family deported to the camps managed to survive. Plenty of others did. But my family members must have been too nice to fight for food scraps, or too weak to survive hard labor, or they didn't know how to cope, or were just plain unlucky. It was said in the camps that the only way out was as smoke through the chimney. I suppose that was the fate of most of my family.

It is a grim heritage that children of the Holocaust survivors deal with in many different ways. Mine was a journey that ranged from early ignorance in a silent household in which the Holocaust was never mentioned; to the realization that there was little a Jew could have done in the face of such a merciless international enterprise of annihilation; to surprise that nevertheless, nobody in my family had the wit to save themselves; and finally, to an understanding of how the murder of my family made me into the person I am, whose default position is to defend the weak.

In my case, I now understand, I did that through my work as a journalist who always sought out the powerless in order to tell their story. Partly because it is in the home of the ignored that real life occurs. And also because the bigger story of society is best told through the tiny stories of the people who make up that society. I have no idea what six million dead really means, but I do know what it means to grow up without relatives. I have no idea what poverty really means, but as the son of refugees, I do know what it is like to be hungry at night.

It is a tenet of journalism: Small story tells big story. And that's where my instincts lay, to meet people who were just trying to get on with their lives. Beaten down, they had no choice but somehow to rise again, to take that next step, however small, into their future.

It is a simple lesson, expressed in simple language, because it is closest to the bone and needs no honeyed words. Small goals. Yet life-changing. After Mohammed Ibrahim lost his wife and five children to starvation, all he wanted was to go home and sit under the tree. All that starving boy in Mogadishu wanted was a pencil. All Odai wanted was to go to the beach. All Wafa, the failed suicide bomber wanted, was to go home. So did Yehona who had lost her parents. Rasha just wanted to play the piano. And maybe Avi got to the heart of the matter because all he wanted was to save a life, which in the Jewish creed means saving the world.

And they do mean the world to me, these people I met along the way, whose stories scratched my soul. Individuals, some brought to their lowest point, others simply confronting daily hardships, all of them wanting so much more from their lives. And what they taught me was how much I already had.

I needed to be reminded of that because of the sense of loss that has always accompanied me. For as I reported on the woes of the world and as people trusted me with their tragic stories, I could never shake the thought that as bad as it was for them, it was worse for my own family. My family had suffered more than any of them, certainly in the sheer number of relatives murdered. That formed the common bond of reporter and subject, me and them. For the response of my mother and father was the same as the people I met on their worst days in Europe, Africa and the Middle East. One small step at a time, one grim day at a time, they too built a better life.

For what choice did they have? Do any of us have?

Fall down seven times, get up eight.

## FINAL THOUGHT

THE PEOPLE IN THESE PAGES affected me greatly, so much so that I don't want to profit from their pain. For this reason I am donating all profits from this book to a charity that supports refugees, not by providing food or clothing but by feeding their souls.

I described my failure to give a starving child a pencil. The young artists of Artolution make up for this a thousandfold by giving paintbrushes and paint to hungry and needy children around the world and teaching them to express themselves through art, bringing some relief and giving some hope.

My role as a journalist is to bear witness and ask questions. Artolution provides answers.

Please learn more at artolution.org and maybe donate to help fund their critical mission.

## ABOUT THE AUTHOR

FOLLOWING A FULL CAREER with the BBC, Reuters and NBC News, during which he won almost every television journalism award, including five Emmys, Martin Fletcher embarked upon his lifelong dream to write books. His second book, *Walking Israel*, won the National Jewish Book Award for non-fiction and his sixth, *Promised Land*, was a finalist in the fiction category. He is the only author to be honored in both categories. Martin and his beloved wife, Hagar, divide their time between the USA, Mexico and Israel.

## ACKNOWLEDGMENTS

WHERE WOULD MY CAREER BE without three remarkable women: Marcia Markland, the inspiring and ultra-perceptive editor of all my books; Mary Laurence Flynn, equally inspiring in all my reporting at NBC News; and Hagar, my wife, inspiring and supportive in every way imaginable. Thank you, ladies! Sincere thanks also to David Hancock and his super-professional team at Morgan James Publishing, who smoothed my entry into Hybrid publishing.

# A free ebook edition is available with the purchase of this book.

**To claim your free ebook edition:**

1. Visit MorganJamesBOGO.com
2. Sign your name CLEARLY in the space
3. Complete the form and submit a photo of the entire copyright page
4. You or your friend can download the ebook to your preferred device

A **FREE** ebook edition is available for you or a friend with the purchase of this print book.

CLEARLY SIGN YOUR NAME ABOVE

**Instructions to claim your free ebook edition:**
1. Visit MorganJamesBOGO.com
2. Sign your name CLEARLY in the space above
3. Complete the form and submit a photo of this entire page
4. You or your friend can download the ebook to your preferred device

## Print & Digital Together Forever.

Snap a photo          Free ebook          Read anywhere

CPSIA information can be obtained
at www.ICGtesting.com
Printed in the USA
JSHW010028060423
39944JS00008B/63

9 781636 981079